THE
CONSUMER'S
GUIDE TO

DOG FOOD

What's in Dog Food, Why It's There and How to Choose the Best Food for Your Dog

LIZ PALIKA

HOWELL
BOOK
HOUSE

New York

Howell Book House

A Simon & Schuster/Macmillan Company
1633 Broadway
New York, NY 10019

Library of Congress Cataloging-in-Publication Data

Palika, Liz, 1954–
    The consumer's guide to dog food : what's in dog food, why it's
there and how to choose the best food for your dog / Liz Palika.
        p. cm
        Includes bibliographical references and index.
    ISBN: 0-87605-467-X
        1. Dogs—Food. 2. Dogs—Nutrition. 3. Consumer education.
I. Title.
    SF427.4.P36   1996
    636.7'085—dc20   96-11579
        CIP

Manufactured in the United States of America
10 9 8 7 6 5 4 3 2 1

CONTENTS

DIRECTORY OF CHARTS

INTRODUCTION

The idea for this book grew out of my efforts to find the "perfect" food for my dogs. Over the years I have owned German Shepherd Dogs, Papillons and Australian Shepherds, as well as a Bulldog, a Doberman Pinscher and a couple of mixed-breed dogs. Several of these dogs had special needs regarding food: a couple had food allergies, two had severe (and I mean severe!) flatulence and one was prone to soft stools. One dog would gain weight just sniffing food, one needed special food as a puppy and a few others ate a senior-type food as they got older.

All of these special circumstances caused me to research dog foods. I wanted to find out what dog food really was, especially as compared to the advertisements. I wanted to know what the differences were between the puppy, adult and senior foods. I needed to learn how to read dog food labels and to decipher the terminology on them.

As I started to understand a little bit more, that small bit of knowledge caused me to ask more and more questions. Why did the dog foods offer such a variety of ingredients? Were some better than others? What was "by-product meal"? Or even stranger, what was "digest"? And most important, can dogs effectively metabolize and use all of these different ingredients? If they did, why did some dog foods cause such large piles of feces in the backyard when other dog foods seemed to have so much less waste?

I also talked to many other concerned dog owners, some with dogs with particular problems and others with healthy dogs, who were concerned about what their dogs ate. I found that many people relied on what other people said about foods: "Oh, so-and-so has been feeding her dog this brand for years." Other people read the labels on foods and tried to make an educated decision. I also found a tremendous amount of misinformation!

At the time I was doing all this research, a friend of mine, Joan Swanson Hamilton, was also researching dog foods. She was raising a couple of puppies, one of which had a problem digesting food properly.

She also had a very old dog that needed special food and a young adult Newfoundland that wasn't keeping weight on.

We shared information as we researched, and we both came to similar conclusions. First, we found that what dogs eat does make a difference. Our dogs' health, activity levels and even mental health seemed to be closely related to their food. Dogs with allergies were affected even more. Joan discovered that her Golden Retriever, Mistich, would break out in a rash with even one beef-basted dog bone. My Australian Shepherd, Care Bear, would start scratching uncontrollably after eating a dog food with wheat as one of the first five ingredients.

We also decided that there is no one perfect food for every dog. Each dog has its own individual nutritional needs and, to make matters worse, those needs can change over the years. The informed dog owner must learn to make an educated decision as to what will work best for that particular dog. That is what Joan and I have done and will continue doing as our dogs' nutritional needs change as they grow up and older.

Throughout my research, I also found, to my dismay, that many experts disagree (sometimes vehemently!) about dog food. One researcher might state one fact, with research to back it up, while another expert will argue exactly the opposite, with research to support those findings. In most of the situations where experts disagree, I have tried to provide you with both sides of the argument so that you, as your dog's owner and as a wise consumer, can make up your own mind.

This book was written to give you the knowledge and tools to feed your dog as best you can. I have provided you with information about nutrition, dog food ingredients (the good, the bad and the awful), how to read dog food labels, how to contact the dog food companies for straight answers, and much, much more.

As you are trying to find the right food for your dog, if you have questions about your dog's health, please contact your veterinarian. This book was read by several veterinarians prior to publication; however, it was not written as a replacement for good veterinary care. Instead, it was written to serve as a tool for you so that you, as an educated, informed dog owner, can participate more fully in your dog's health, well-being and longevity.

Liz Palika
and my constant companions and very willing dog food test
participants, Care Bear, Ursa and Dax, Australian Shepherds.
June 1995

ONE

DOG FOOD: WHERE IT'S BEEN AND WHERE IT'S GOING

Researchers believe that dogs and mankind have been companions for as long as 15,000 to 20,000 years. The exact time is, of course, hard to pinpoint, but dogs have been found in cave paintings, ancient artworks and grave sites, all of which give us a rough estimate of the length of the relationship. One question that is not answered by ancient artworks is why the two species were attracted to each other in the first place. After all, wolves are and were predators, and other than his brain and the tools he could fashion, early man was virtually unarmed. The ancestors to today's dogs probably found early man to be an easy target, especially the very young and the very old.

At some point, however, perhaps during a very hard winter, one or two wolves must have found it was easier to scavenge from early man's butchering sites than it was to hunt entirely on their own. From that point on, for those particular wolves, mankind became associated with food and, after all, food was and still is survival. Individual wolves might then have started to follow men back to their caves or, as they changed territories, might have shown other wolves how easy it was to find food after men had hunted.

From here, many things must have happened to show wolves (and men) that mutual cooperation would benefit both species. As this cooperation developed, companionship became part of the relationship, as did mutual protection. However, the first step in the relationship was most certainly food.

Since those early years, dogs have fed mankind by hunting game, protecting crops and livestock from vermin, retrieving birds and herding and protecting domestic animals. In return, mankind has provided domesticated dogs with food. But it has not always been an equal bargain.

FROM SCAVENGER TO PARTNER

As dogs became domesticated over thousands of years, they ate the leftovers: the scraps left from butchering game or the food left after a meal. Almost certainly, the dogs supplemented their given food by hunting or scavenging on their own. A mouse or a rabbit, fallen fruit, scraps of hide or bits of bone from an earlier kill could all help fill an empty stomach.

However, as mankind itself evolved and progressed and as the value of dogs became more apparent, the food given to dogs changed. Food that had value to people—meat, fish, cooked grains and fruit—was shared with dogs. This was often a sacrifice on the part of the dog's owner because the difference between life or death was, as noted earlier, often the amount of food available.

The Inuit (Eskimo) people shared their food with their dogs, even when food was in short supply. However, in times of starvation, when people were dying, dogs starved too and were often eaten, except for one or two dogs that were purposely saved as future breeding stock.

DIFFERENT FOODS FOR DIFFERENT DOGS

As the partnership between mankind and domestic dogs progressed and became more specialized, different breeds of dogs came about. Some were created by geographical isolation; others were bred for specific working instincts and others for looks, coat type, color or a myriad of other reasons. Just as people of different cultures the world over ate different foods or similar foods prepared in different ways, so, too, did those people's dogs. The Inuits' dogs ate fish, seal meat and blubber and thrived on that. Greyhounds ate rabbit or antelope, and the ancestors of today's British herding dogs ate mutton and potatoes. Again, as throughout history, dogs ate what their owners ate—the food that was available and affordable.

THE FIRST COMMERCIAL FOODS

The first known commercial dog foods were prepared in England from the carcasses of horses that died in harness on London streets. Butchers would sell the leftovers—entrails, brains and other scraps—

packaged especially for pet food. In 1870, Spratt's Patent Meal Fibrine Dog Cakes became available, and although it was fed to the dogs in the British Royal Kennels, it was considered a luxury for most dog owners and never really became popular.

DOG FOOD IN AMERICA

In 1926, the Purina Company established the Pet Care Center for testing new animal foods, including dog foods. Purina's Dog Chow Checkers, a pelleted dry food, was introduced as a "nutritionally adequate ration for reproduction and growth," the first commercially available dog food to make such a claim. Since Purina already had a reputation for producing good food for domestic animals, especially swine, people were willing to give the dog food a try.

Purina's claim was put to the test in 1933 when Admiral Richard Byrd was preparing for his second Antarctic expedition. Teams of dogs were going to be used as transportation and Admiral Byrd wanted the dogs to be in the best shape possible. He asked nutritionists from Massachusetts General Hospital to recommend the best food available; their choice was Purina's Dog Chow Checkers. Two years of hard work later, the dogs were still thriving.

In 1929, the Albers Brothers Milling Company produced a limited amount of dog food, a meat meal and gruel mixture. It was shipped to Alaska where it was cooked with fish prior to feeding sled dogs. Later, the company merged with Carnation, which went on to establish a kennel of purebred dogs to test their new dog foods.

In 1936, Carnation made its new Friskies dog foods available to the public. Alfred Gromley, the president of Albers Brothers Milling Company, said in 1939, "For the first time, Friskies brings owners a cube-type food that is a complete ration for dogs." Father Bernard Hubbard, "the Glacier Priest," depended on Friskies dog food to feed his team of Huskies as he traveled throughout Alaska, visiting the Eskimo people. He believed so strongly in the food that he brought extra to share with his hosts' dogs.

A NEW CONVENIENCE

Although manufacturers in both England and the United States continued to produce and sell prepared dog foods in the late 1800s and early 1900s, it wasn't until after World War II that the idea really caught on. Prepared dog food was a convenience, just like drive-through restaurants and frozen dinners, and such conveniences were much sought after by American women after the war.

Most of the early dog foods were meat-based foods, usually beef or horsemeat. Meat scraps were readily available and inexpensive, and it was widely believed by dog owners that as carnivores, dogs should eat meat. Although many grains and other nonmeat sources of nutrition were available to dog food manufacturers, often at a cheaper cost than meat, these ingredients were not often used since it was known by researchers of the time that dogs do not have the necessary digestive enzymes to break down the crude fiber or cellulose present in grains, beans, seeds and many vegetables. Dry dog foods did make a significant gain over canned foods during World War II, due to the shortage of metals and, consequently, the tins in which to package wet foods. However, the quality and digestibility of the dry foods was often in question.

THE EXTRUSION PROCESS

In 1956, a research team working for the Purina Company developed a controllable cooking process called extrusion. Extrusion cooking allowed feed grains to be used in dog and cat foods for the first time. Dr. Thomas Willard, a nutritional consultant, wrote in a July 1992 *AKC Gazette* article, "What Are We Really Feeding Our Dogs?": "Extrusion cooking adds a crunchy texture to the food for better palatability, and is the single most important development in the pet food industry since man first tossed a wild canine a bone over 20,000 years ago."

WHAT IS THE EXTRUSION PROCESS?

Commercial pet food manufacturers use the extrusion process to cook and form their dry foods. Ingredients like grains and meats come to the manufacturers in an already dry form and are loaded into an extruder. Enough moisture is added to cook the ingredients, which are brought up to the desired temperature. The extruder pushes the food through the machine with the help of steam and pressure. The food is then passed through a plate branded with the shape of the kibble, and sliced to size. Because of the temperature of the food and the pressure under which it is being extruded, when the kibble hits the air it expands slightly. You can sometimes see the air holes in extruded kibble. From this stage, the food is usually coated with a flavor enhancer.

By the mid-1960s, prepackaged dog food had become big business in the United States, and over $750 million was spent annually on dog food—twice what was spent on baby food! By the mid-1970s, dog and cat food combined was a $1.75 billion industry. *Petfood Industry* magazine reported, in its July/August 1994 issue, that sales of dog foods in 1993 reached $4,990 million—almost $5 billion! (See Chapter Six, Figure 18.)

SATISFYING DOGS AND THEIR OWNERS

Rick Shields, Ph.D., is associate director of nutrition for Quaker Oats/Ken-L Ration/Gaines dog foods. In "From Concept to Can" by Amy Shojai (*AKC Gazette*, October 1994), Shields said that dog foods must satisfy two consumers: the dog and its owner.

Many health-conscious dog owners want to share their philosophical beliefs with their dogs and may require that their dogs eat a vegetarian diet or a food containing no by-products or preservatives. Other dog owners have different requirements, wanting their dogs to eat an all-beef food or a free-range chicken food. Some of these consumer needs are based on a desire to feed a treasured pet the best food possible. Other desires can be unrealistic; however, many dog food manufacturers have striven to meet as many of these needs as possible, hence the variety of foods available.

Dog food manufacturers appeal to dog owners in other ways, too. The look and smell of a dog food is primarily for the owner's benefit. Dogs don't care what the food looks like, but dog owners want the food to look fresh and smell acceptable. Dog foods that come in tiny bone shapes and bright, meaty colors are made so strictly for the owner.

The other consumer is the dog. A food that is not eaten will certainly not benefit the dog in any way. Of course, many hungry dogs will eat anything placed in front of them, but owners notice when the dog is reluctant to eat or is not gobbling the food with its normal relish.

WHAT COMPANIES WANT

Dog food manufacturers have spent considerable time and money researching dog foods and developing new foods with four goals:

1. to meet the needs of the dog's owner;
2. to make a food the dog will want to eat;
3. to make a food to meet the dog's nutritional needs; and
4. to make a profit.

RESEARCH AND MORE RESEARCH

The development of a dog food is usually years in the making. Many factors come into play: What is the purpose or goal of this new food? Is it going to target a specific population, such as geriatric dogs or puppies? What are the proposed ingredients for this diet? Are the ingredients readily available? What would the cost of these ingredients be?

When a recipe or a combination of ingredients is proposed for a new food, the ingredients must then be analyzed. What is the nutritional value of each ingredient and how do they work together? Will these ingredients meet or surpass the nutritional needs of the dogs being fed?

Other factors in the recipe must also be researched. In what order should the ingredients be added? How long should the ingredients be cooked and at what temperatures?

When test batches of the new food have been produced, the food is again sent back to the laboratory for more analysis and final testing. Once the food has passed this stage, it is then produced in limited quantities for palatability tests.

TESTING WHERE IT COUNTS: ON THE DOGS

The Ralston Purina and Carnation companies established feeding research centers earlier, but other dog food manufacturers maintain kennels, too, including the Iams Company, another giant in the dog food industry. Some dog food manufacturers ask breeders, veterinarians or kennels to test new foods. The goal is to make sure the dog will eagerly eat the food being offered.

At the Iams Animal Care Center, new foods are tested for **palatability** by giving the dog two bowls, each containing a different food. Technicians note which food was eaten first, which bowl was emptied first and if any food was left over, which one. The next day, the same test is repeated, except the foods are in different positions so the dog doesn't develop the habit of eating one particular bowl first. Because a new food may attract a dog simply because it is different, the tests are repeated for several days to make sure the food has "staying power."

The food is also tested by many dogs. Some dogs, such as Labrador Retrievers and Beagles, will eat just about anything. Other breeds and individual dogs are more finicky. Therefore, most of the care centers operated by dog food manufacturers keep several different breeds, usually a selection of small, medium and large size breeds. The Iams Company keeps ten breeds of different sizes and heritages; the Ralston Purina company keeps Beagles, Labrador Retrievers and Siberian Huskies. Quaker Oats/Ken-L Ration/Gaines has Beagles, Labrador Retrievers, Boxers, Fox Terriers and Poodles.

If the food does not seem to be readily accepted by most of the dogs, it goes back to the laboratory for more work. Jeff Bennett, owner of Nature's Recipe dog foods, said, "We may 'tweak' or modify a dog food formula three to five times to get the palatability where we think it should be."

DIGESTIBILITY. When the recipe for the new food has been tested for palatability and found acceptable, the food is then tested for digestibility. The dogs' feces are analyzed, with the nutritional value of the food compared to the nutritional content of the feces. Other tests analyze the dogs' urine, again determining what nutrients were excreted. With these tests, technicians can determine how much nutritional value the dog is actually getting from the food.

LONG-TERM FEEDING TESTS. Once the new food makes it this far, it is then fed to various dogs for a period of time and accurate records are kept as to the dogs' health and well-being. Depending upon the target of the new food, it may be fed to puppies, a nursing dam, active adults or geriatric dogs.

Control studies are often done, comparing similar dogs fed a known diet to dogs fed the new diet. Researchers measure body weight, blood profiles, bone growth, skin and coat condition and general health.

These tests may take from six to nine months, or even as long as two years. Foods that will eventually be targeted to specific dogs, such as allergic dogs or geriatric dogs, must have additional tests to back up those claims, and that takes time.

DOG FOOD REGULATORS

THE AMERICAN ASSOCIATION OF FEED CONTROL OFFICIALS. The American Association of Feed Control Officials (AAFCO) was formed to develop standards for domestic animal foods. The association is made up of feed control officials from all 50 states. Although the organization has no enforcement powers, reputable companies follow the nutritional, testing and labeling guidelines established by AAFCO. Foods that meet or surpass AAFCO's guidelines usually state so somewhere on the food's label. You can contact the AAFCO at the Georgia Department of Agriculture, Capitol Square, Atlanta, GA 30334.

THE PET FOOD INSTITUTE. The Pet Food Institute was formed in 1958 as the national trade association for pet food manufacturers. The Institute acts as a liaison for the industry before legislative bodies, including the U.S. Department of Agriculture, the Food and Drug Administration, the Federal Trade Commission, the American Association of Feed Control Officials and the United States Congress. By providing accurate information to these and other groups, the Institute strives to promote understanding of the role of pets in our society and the role the pet food industry plays.

In 1992, the Institute introduced the Nutrition Assurance Program (NAP). This is a self-enforcement program designed to give an added assurance of quality nutrition in dog (and other pet) foods. The Institute has established guidelines for feeding tests for foods; once these feeding tests have been completed according to the NAP guidelines, the food will have on its label a statement to the effect that the food is "Complete and balanced nutrition according to AAFCO procedures." If you have a question about a particular food, you can write the Institute at 1200 19th Street NW, Suite 300, Washington, DC 20036, or call 1-800-851-0769.

NATIONAL RESEARCH COUNCIL. The National Research Council (NRC) has established minimum requirements for canine nutrition similar to the Recommended Dietary Allowances (RDAs) for people.

These guidelines are for an "average" dog, but the NRC qualifies its guidelines by stating that these values cannot be taken as an absolute for any individual dog or breed of dog since needs vary with age, activity, body condition, climate, stress levels and temperament.

OTHER WATCHDOG AGENCIES. A number of other agencies have their proverbial paw in dog food testing, manufacturing and labeling. The U.S. Department of Agriculture watches dog food processing. The Food and Drug Administration must approve the artificial flavors, colors and preservatives that might be added to dog foods. The Federal Trade Commission regulates and polices dog food labels. Regulation also happens on a state level with agencies supervising pet food manufacturing, processing and transportation.

THE PRODUCT BEHIND THE PACKAGE

You, as the wise consumer, must keep in mind that dog food companies are also in business to make a profit, and those profits are readily available. Dog foods are big business, taking up more supermarket shelf space than baby food—and only a fraction of the dog food manufacturers in business today even sell their foods in supermarkets. Most manufacturers sell their foods through pet stores, especially the giant chains such as Petco and Pet Supply Warehouse. Other companies sell only to veterinarians.

Advertising dog food is also big business. We have all seen big-name movie or television stars promoting brands of dog food. Breeders and veterinarians tell us about the dog food their dogs prefer. Dogs of all shapes, sizes, breeds and breed mixtures fill our television screens while they demonstrate their love of a certain brand of dog food. Other ads show the love dogs and people have for each other, striving for that "Ooooh!" reaction and hoping the name of that dog food will stick in our minds the next time we go shopping.

No matter where the food is sold or how it is advertised, dog food is a multi-million-dollar business, and each company's goal is to get you, as the dog owner, to buy their food. As the wise consumer, you must be knowledgeable enough to choose the dog food that will best suit your dog's needs.

HOW MUCH WE SPEND ON DOG FOOD

Dog Food Form	Millions of Dollars Sold
Dry foods	$2,532,000
Canned foods	1,215,000
Soft-dry/Semimoist	279,000
Treats	964,000

Total **$4,990,000**

FIGURE 1
AAFCO NUTRIENT PROFILES FOR DOG FOODS

Nutrient	Units	Growth Foods	Adult/ Maint	Maximum
	DM **	(Minimum)	(Minimum)	
Protein	%	22.0	18.0	
Arginine	%	.62	.51	
Histidine	%	.22	.18	
Isoleucine	%	.45	.37	
Leucine	%	.72	.59	
Lysine	%	.77	.63	
Methionine-cysteine	%	.53	.43	
Phenylalanine-tyrosine	%	.89	.73	
Threonine	%	.58	.48	
Tryptophan	%	.20	.16	
Valine	%	.48	.39	
Fat	%	8.0	5.0	
Linoleic acid	%	1.0	1.0	
Minerals				
Calcium	%	1.0	.6	2.5
Phosphorus	%	.8	.5	1.6
Ca:P ratio		1:1	1:1	2:1
Potassium	%	.6	.6	

| Nutrient | Units | Growth Foods | Adult/ Maint | Maximum |
	DM **	(Minimum)	(Minimum)	
Sodium	%	.3	.06	
Chloride	%	.45	.09	
Magnesium	%	.04	.04	.3
Iron	mg/kg	80	80	3000
Copper	mg/kg	7.3	7.3	250
Manganese	mg/kg	5.0	5.0	
Zinc	mg/kg	120	120	1000
Iodine	mg/kg	1.5	1.5	50
Selenium	mg/kg	.11	.11	2
Vitamins				
Vitamin A	IU/kg	5000	5000	50,000
Vitamin D	IU/kg	500	500	5000
Vitamin E	IU/kg	50	50	1000
Thiamine	mg/kg	1.0	1.0	
Riboflavin	mg/kg	2.2	2.2	
Pantothenic acid	mg/kg	10	10	
Niacin	mg/kg	11.4	11.4	
Pyridoxine	mg/kg	1.0	1.0	
Folic acid	mg/kg	.18	.18	
Vitamin B12	mg/kg	.022	.022	
Choline	mg/kg	1200	1200	

**Note: The units in this table are expressed on a dry matter (DM) basis. Before comparing them to the labels on a particular dog food, adjust them for the percentage of dry matter in the food. See Chapter Five, Figure 13 for the formula for this conversion.

TWO

NUTRITION: WHAT'S IN DOG FOOD AND WHY

Throughout history, food in its various forms has been used as medicine. Did your grandmother give you chicken soup when you were sick? Almost all human cultures have a number of foods—not just herbs, but everyday foods—that are recommended for certain circumstances. Over the years, these "old wives' tales" have been replaced by modern medicine. Modern medicine developed certain "magic bullets"—aspirin, antibiotics and so on—and, in the process, forgot much of the ancient wisdom by which mankind survived for thousands of years.

THE PRICE OF PROCESSED FOODS

These magic bullets have indeed increased longevity and cured many diseases, but at what cost? People and their domestic animals are suffering from malnutrition at drastically increased rates and many researchers feel that our overly processed foods are to blame. We are, literally, cooking the nutrients out of our foods. Other researchers are recognizing many more food allergies than were previously known, both in people and in dogs, and feel that this is also due to our reliance on processed foods.

We have forgotten many of the lessons those "old wives" taught us about foods and herbs and how to use them to create and maintain good health, rather than relying on magic bullets to cure existing problems. However, in more recent years, researchers, nutritionists and alternative medicine practitioners have found that many of these old remedies are based in fact: Many foods do have medicinal properties and these properties should be a part of good daily nutrition.

This attitude toward food emphasizes its importance, for without food, we would die. With a poor diet, one that does not meet our nutritional needs, we may live, but we will not live as long or as well. With a good diet that does satisfy our nutritional needs, our odds of living better are drastically increased. The same applies to our dogs.

GOOD FOOD = GOOD HEALTH

Before you go shopping for dog food, it is vital that you have an understanding of good nutrition and how it affects your dog's health. Good nutrition is needed for reproduction, lactation and normal growth. Food supplies the needed substances that act as regulators for the body's many processes, including organ development and functions. Food is necessary for disease resistance, for healing and as a source of energy so that the dog can function and live from day to day.

Nutrition is the relationship between food and the health of the body. The body—in this case, your dog's—takes in food and digests it through chemical changes. Dogs are considered to be remnant carnivores. In other words, dogs have sharp, flesh-tearing teeth; a simple stomach and short digestive tract; and the absence of the saliva enzyme amylase (which predigests starch), all characteristic of carnivores.

Carnivores, by definition, eat meat. Meat, or animal protein, is more easily digested by dogs than protein obtained from other sources. However, even carnivores eat vegetables and grains. Wild dogs, coyotes and wolves often ingest the partially digested plant products found in the entrails of their prey. Carnivores are also opportunists, eating anything that is available, including berries and fruits.

THE DIGESTIVE PROCESS

All foods eaten by the dog must be broken down by the body into simpler chemical forms. This process is called digestion. With dogs, active digestion starts in the stomach, where food is mixed with gastric juices containing enzymes that break up protein, fat, carbohydrates and other substances.

As the food passes into the **small intestine** from the stomach, some of the food, which is now changing into simpler chemical forms, is absorbed by the body. Depending upon the nutrient, some of the food is absorbed by the bloodstream through tiny blood vessels in the small intestine. Other nutrients are channeled through the **lymph system**.

During this part of digestion, water-soluble vitamins are picked up by the bloodstream.

The **liver** also plays an important part in the digestive process by changing some of the nutrients into products needed by the individual cells. Other nutrients are stored by the liver for future use.

The dog is now metabolizing some of its food. Lavon J. Dunne wrote in the *Nutrition Almanac* (3rd Ed.), "The process of metabolism involves all of the chemical changes that nutrients undergo from the time they are absorbed until they become part of the body or are excreted from the body." Those chemical changes can be incredibly complex. The body is constantly working with these nutrients, constructing body chemicals such as blood, enzymes and hormones, or breaking down compounds to supply the cells or body with energy.

The feces excreted by the dog are body wastes; i.e., normal waste material produced by the dog's body plus undigested food material. When digestibility studies are undertaken to analyze the digestibility of a particular food, the feces are analyzed. The formula is the amount

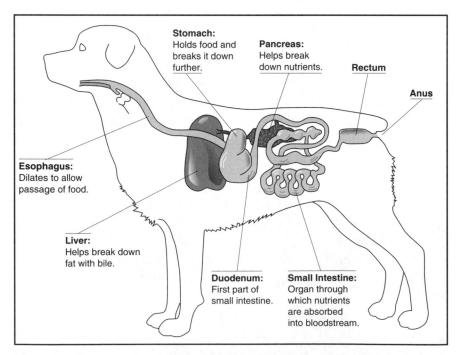

The canine digestive system, and the functions of the various organs involved.

of nutrients ingested minus the amount of nutrients in feces, which equals the apparent digestibility of the food.

FACTORS AFFECTING GOOD NUTRITION

Proper nutrition, for dogs, means that all of the body's essential nutrients are being supplied by the food being eaten. Those needs include appropriate amounts of protein, fat, carbohydrates, vitamins, minerals and, of course, water.

Each individual dog, of every breed, will have slightly different needs for good nutrition. Things that affect nutrition include:

- the dog's age
- its heritage
- its state of general health
- whether or not it is being used in a breeding program
- its work or exercise requirements
- climate
- stress levels
- the food it is eating

AGE. Nutritional needs vary dramatically with the dog's age. Rapidly growing puppies require significantly higher protein levels than do adult or older dogs. The American Association of Feed Control Officials (AAFCO) Nutrient Profiles for Dog Foods (see Chapter One, Figure 1) show that puppies should eat a food with protein levels no lower than 22 percent, compared to 18 percent for adult dogs. In comparison, the senior or geriatric dog with weak or diseased kidneys will require even less protein than an adult dog and should eat less fat, too, so that the kidneys are not stressed by more protein than they can handle.

HERITAGE. Just as the different breeds of dogs developed different coat lengths and types, body shapes and instincts, so, too, did many breeds develop different nutritional needs. Some breeds will willingly eat and thrive on a fish diet, while others do better with more beef or mutton.

William Cusick, author of *Choosing the Best Food for Your Breed of Dog* (Adele Publications, 1990), states, "The length of time needed to make a nutritional requirement change due to exposure to a new environment's food supply can take thousands of years." He goes on to say that each breed of dog has retained the genetic differences that it developed in its native environment and would, therefore, do better on a diet that more closely resembled its native food.

Breeds, too, often have different inherited problems or needs regarding nutrition. Many Dalmatian breeders recommend feeding their breed a low-purine diet to help with the breed's problem with uric acid metabolism. Alaskan Malamutes often have a problem metabolizing zinc, Bedlington Terriers have problems with copper and Giant Schnauzers often have a vitamin B12 deficiency. All of these things have a bearing upon the dog's nutritional health.

GENERAL HEALTH. Nutritional needs can vary dramatically depending upon the dog's health. A dog stressed by injury or disease will need more support from a good food to enable healing. A dog that is carrying a heavy load of parasites, either internal (roundworms, hookworms, etc.) or external (fleas or ticks), will need medical attention to fight off the parasites and will also need nutritional support to regain good health. Good nutrition can also work toward preventing many health problems by helping to keep the immune system running properly.

REPRODUCTION. Good nutrition is necessary for both the stud dog and the brood bitch prior to breeding. A stud dog that is not well nourished may not produce viable sperm and may even have a reduced desire to breed.

If the brood bitch is not well nourished, she may not ovulate properly, may not release eggs or may not have the reserves herself to adequately nourish the growing embryos. During both gestation and lactation, the brood bitch will be robbing her own body of nutrition to satisfy the growing puppies' needs. It's important that her state of health prior to breeding is good and that her nutritional needs are met before breeding, during gestation and during lactation.

WORK AND EXERCISE. Most breeds of dogs were designed, at some point, to do a job. Some breeds herded sheep or cattle and others guarded their owners' property while other breeds retrieved birds. To do the job they were designed to do, they needed to be physically active. Granted, some breeds were and still are more active than others, but all needed to be active enough to do their work. Although many of these breeds (and individual dogs) are no longer performing their ancient tasks, some still are, and need the nutritional support to do so.

Even dogs that no longer work hard on a daily basis should get regular exercise. Exercise stimulates digestion, strengthens blood vessels and muscles, imparts vigor to all of the body's organs and increases the body's need for good nutrition. A dog that works, runs or plays hard will need an increase in energy (calories) to keep up the activity.

CLIMATE. The climate in which the dog lives, works and plays will have considerable bearing on its nutritional needs. In cold weather, the dog may need twice the calories needed in warmer weather, both because it needs the extra calories to keep warm and because it will probably be more active when it is colder.

STRESS. Stress can be many things to a dog; it can be the move to a new home, the addition of a new family member, increased activity, new training or dog show competition. Dogs facing stress on a daily basis for any period of time should have a diet with slightly higher protein levels.

FOOD. The food that your dog is eating can cause stress, too, especially if the food is of poor quality, is made up of ingredients that are not easily digestible or is simply not the right food for your dog. Food can also cause problems if the dog's diet is abruptly changed, which can cause gastrointestinal disorders and diarrhea. Too much or too little food can be a problem, too, for obvious reasons.

FOOD AND THE BODY

There is no single thing that can ensure good health. Good health is a jigsaw puzzle with many pieces to it. Regular daily exercise, emotional security and adequate rest are pieces of the puzzle. Heredity certainly is a part of the puzzle; a dog that is descended from healthy, sound parents and grandparents will have more of a chance of good health. An environment relatively free of physical dangers, excess chemicals and insecticides will also aid in the maintenance of good health. And, of course, good nutrition is an important part of the puzzle.

Your dog's immune system is a marvel, even to researchers who spend their careers studying it. The immune system is an army that fights viruses, bacteria and disease. Every breath brings with it potentially deadly warriors, ready to strike, as does the dirt in the backyard or the water sitting out in an open dish. Even your dog's old chew toy in the backyard is covered with bacteria that could, without a healthy immune system, cause untold trouble.

An immune system can be weakened by inadequate nutrition, and this can lead to a variety of disorders or can make existing disorders more serious. On the other hand, a strong immune system, backed up by a good, healthy diet, can fight existing diseases and can work alongside medical treatments prescribed by your dog's veterinarian.

ALLERGIES AND FOOD

Canine allergies are just as common as human allergies. If your neighbor's bushes are flowering, you might be sneezing, but your dog might be scratching itself raw. Allergies are a case of the immune system overreacting. The immune system recognizes an antigen (a foreign substance) and produces antibodies to fight it. When it recognizes that substance again, it overreacts and an allergic response is the result.

Some allergies are *inhalant*: the allergen is inhaled during breathing. Other allergies are *contact* allergies, caused (as the name implies) by contact with the allergen, such as grass. Still other allergies might be caused by *food*. Food allergies may cause an instant response with swelling of the mouth or throat, or there may be a more delayed reaction, such as gas and bloating that appear a few hours later. Even more delayed reactions, appearing days after ingesting the wrong food, are common but less recognized because they are harder to pinpoint.

Christine Wilford, DVM, stated in her *Dog Fancy* magazine article "Allergies" (May 1994) that up to 60 percent of all dogs with nonseasonal allergic skin disease suffer from food allergies. The most common ingredients causing problems are beef, milk, wheat, soy and artificial food additives.

Food allergies may show up as small red bumps that cause the dog to scratch and bite at itself, damaging the skin and leaving it open to secondary infections. With food allergies, the skin may itch all over, but the most common areas of sensitivity are the feet and ears; in fact, paws stained red by saliva are a common indicator of food allergies.

These are not the only symptoms of food allergies, though; they're just the most common. Other symptoms include joint pain and stiffness; epilepsy; weakness; fatigue; bowel disease, including poor or loose stools or mucus in stools; kidney inflammation; and kidney disease. Dogs with food allergies can also suffer from many behavior problems, including hyperactivity, anxiety, fear, depression and restlessness, although the most common is aggressive behavior.

Theron Randolph, MD, a physician and researcher, stated that hidden or delayed-onset food allergies are "the most common undiagnosed illness in medicine today." Diagnosis may be made through blood tests or feeding trials. In either case, if you suspect a food allergy, contact your veterinarian.

CANCER AND FOOD

Cancer is a word that strikes terror into the hearts of many people. There is much researchers know about cancer and much more that is not known. We know that cancer cells can grow very rapidly, can create their own blood supply and can invade local tissues. Books have been written about the various types of cancers, but using very simple definitions, these abnormal growths are called tumors. Those that are relatively harmless are said to be benign; those that spread and damage surrounding tissues are said to be malignant.

Many researchers believe that every living body (human, canine and otherwise) has some cancer cells. Normally, the body's immune system reacts to these cells and either destroys them, inhibits their spread or in some other, unknown manner, prevents them from forming tumors. Cancer results when the immune system, for whatever reason, fails to react to the forming cells.

Dr. Gregory Ogilvie, DVM, of Colorado State University College of Veterinary Medicine and Biomedical Sciences, has found that cancer changes the way a dog uses, or metabolizes, nutrients. In a three-year study, dogs treated for lymphoma with conventional chemotherapy were fed a special diet. The diet didn't cure the lymphoma, but it did extend life for anywhere between nine months and three years.

Susan Donoghue, VMD, is a board-certified nutritionist. In her April 1994 *AKC Gazette* column, "Nutrition: Cancer Prevention and Treatment," Donoghue discussed a Boxer undergoing treatment for cancer. "We gradually introduced a premium, canned, meat-based grocery dog food to the Boxer's diet. As the cancer treatment progressed and the dog's· appetite waned, he was offered a highly palatable chicken, liver and rice homemade diet." She continued by saying that the Boxer was then offered liquid enterals, such as Ensure, which offer very high quality nutrition.

Unfortunately, there are no known foods that will cure cancer in dogs, and the only prevention is to make sure the dog is eating a nutritious diet that will keep the immune system strong and healthy.

DENTAL HEALTH

By the age of three years, 80 percent of all dogs have dental disease. Dental disease is more than just bad breath; it also means gum damage and tooth loss and, if it progresses, even heart and kidney damage. Regular at-home dental care (brushing) can help prevent early dental problems, but veterinary check-ups are needed, too, especially for older dogs.

Although what the dog eats will not eliminate dental problems, a good diet can help in a couple of ways. First, good nutrition will help the immune system cope; and second, hard kibbles or biscuits help scrape food particles off the teeth.

GASTROINTESTINAL DISORDERS

Gastrointestinal disorders can be caused by a variety of problems, including parasites, infections, metabolic imbalances, tumors, injuries or allergies. Dogs that raid the garbage can and ingest meat wrappers, sandwich leftovers and apple cores (among other things) usually end up with gastrointestinal disorders. However, the most common causes of this malady are usually related to food; specifically, changing foods too quickly, feeding spoiled or poor-quality food, or feeding the dog a food that it cannot metabolize properly.

A dog's brand or type of food should never be changed abruptly, as rapid changes inevitably result in an upset stomach, vomiting and diarrhea.

CHANGING YOUR DOG'S FOOD

Ideally, changing brands of food or other components of your dog's diet should take place over a period of three weeks. The dog should eat one-quarter (25 percent) of the new food and three-quarters (75 percent) of its old food for one week. The second week the food can be 50/50: half the old food and half the new food. During the third week, the dog can eat three-quarters new food and one-quarter its old food. By the fourth week, the dog should be eating its new food with little or no gastrointestinal upset.

Although some dogs seem to have cast-iron stomachs that can handle anything and everything, many dogs will become ill when they eat spoiled food, especially when raiding the trash can or when eating a spoiled dog food or a dog food made from inferior ingredients. Years ago, it was common practice to feed dogs raw meat; however, researchers now know that raw meat—even meat sold for human consumption—can contain pathogenic bacteria that can seriously endanger good health.

Even though what the dog eats can often be the cause of gastrointestinal disorders, a good diet can also act to help heal these same disorders. Rice is very easily digested by most dogs and is very bland and soothing to the digestive tract. For this reason, it is the most commonly recommended diet for dogs with gastrointestinal disorders. Usually boiled meat such as ground turkey or lamb is added to the rice for both taste and protein. This diet is not for long-term use, but instead is for feeding until the dog's intestinal tract is functioning normally again.

BLOAT AND GASTRIC DILATATION VOLVULUS

Gastric Dilatation Volvulus (GDV), or "bloat" as it is commonly known, is a potentially fatal disorder that begins when gas or frothy material causes the stomach to expand. This expansion makes it difficult or impossible for the dog to vomit or to pass food or gas from the stomach to the intestinal tract. In severe cases, the stomach may rotate, causing shock, organ failure and death.

Although GDV is more often seen in large, deep-chested breeds of dogs such as Great Danes, Akitas, German Shepherd Dogs and Irish Setters, other breeds are not immune.

Researchers have been studying GDV and think that many factors lead to the disorder, including the shape and angle of the digestive tract, stretching of the ligaments that hold the stomach in place, too much exercise after eating, gulping of water after eating and some dog food ingredients.

In recent years, soy and soy products have been blamed as contributing factors to GDV. However, a study undertaken at the Virginia-Maryland College of Veterinary Medicine found that dry, soy-based dog foods were no more likely to cause bloat than foods not containing soy. Instead, the researchers concluded that dogs that gulped their water, swallowing quantities of air, were more likely to develop GDV than dogs that lapped their water.

Researchers continue to say, however, that dog owners should avoid rapid food changes (which could trigger gastrointestinal upsets) and should provide a quiet place for the dog to eat undisturbed. Exercise prior to and immediately following mealtimes should be avoided. If there is GDV in your dog's family or if you feel your dog may be at risk, talk to your veterinarian.

HIP DYSPLASIA AND FOOD

Hip dysplasia is a deformity of the hip socket that can be crippling. Fred Lanting, the noted German Shepherd Dog fancier and author of *Canine Hip Dysplasia and Other Orthopedic Problems* (Alpine Publishing, 1980), said, "Hip dysplasia occurs in most domestic species, including man." Lanting feels that diet can play a part in the development of hip dysplasia when genetically predisposed puppies are overfed, get too heavy too quickly and develop too fast. Other researchers agree and recommend a good puppy diet with 20 to 24 percent protein. The same researchers discourage oversupplementation with calcium and vitamin D, stating that these supplements can skew the balance of nutrients in the food and lead to more orthopedic problems.

THE EFFECTS OF THYROID

Hyperthyroidism is the overproduction of hormones by the thyroid gland. Symptoms might include nervousness, fatigue, weight loss and rapid pulse. **Hypothyroidism** is the underproduction of hormones, and results in decreased appetite, dull dry coat, clumsiness, lack of vigor and, in breeding male dogs, lowered sperm count.

Although both types of thyroid disease can be inherited, nutrition can also be a factor. A study performed in the mid-1980s by Akita breeders showed a tendency toward thyroid problems in dogs eating a dry dog food high in soybeans and soybean meal. Soybeans are an incomplete protein source, lacking several essential amino acids. (See Chapter Three.) This could potentially lead to a lack of tyrosine, the amino acid that stimulates the thyroid gland to produce more hormones. Although additional studies are needed, dogs with diagnosed thyroid disease, or a genetic predisposition to it, should avoid foods high in soy.

EATING RIGHT FOR A LIFETIME

Although many things contribute to how long a dog will live, including heredity, environment and general health, good nutrition has been linked by several studies to longevity. A diet that supplies the dog's nutritional needs is imperative to good health, which in turn goes hand in hand with a long life.

FIGURE 2
DOG FOOD MANUFACTURERS' 800 NUMBERS

Alpo	800-366-6033
ANF	800-489-2770
Booda	800-824-9897
Friskies Pet Care Company	800-682-7217
Fromm	800-325-6331
Gereen	800-358-4908
Happy Jack	800-326-5225
Hill's Pet Nutrition Science Diet	800-445-5777
Iams	800-525-4267
Joy	800-245-4125
Kal Kan	800-525-5273
Kruse's Country Perfection	800-854-1781
Merit Dog Foods	800-265-6323
Nabisco	800-NABISCO
Natural Life Pet Products	800-367-2391
Nutro	800-833-5330
Pet Products Plus	800-592-6687
Precise	800-446-7148
Premium Life Span	800-874-3221
Quaker Oats/Ken-L Ration	800-4MY-PETS
Ralston Purina	800-778-7462
Sensible Choice	800-592-6687
Super Pro	800-227-0411
Techni-Cal	800-265-3370
Technomene Pet Foods Proper Balance	800-982-9802
Vet's Choice Select Balance	800-494-PETS
Walthum	800-525-5273

THREE

THE BASIC BUILDING
BLOCKS OF FOOD

There are eight basic building blocks of nutrition that should be present in the food your dog eats. They are

- water
- enzymes
- protein
- carbohydrates
- fats
- fiber
- vitamins
- minerals

These nutrients contain chemical substances that affect the body. They might provide the body with energy or might assist in the regulation of body processes, or they might provide for the growth and repair of tissues.

Each of these nutrient building blocks has its own purpose and function, but it does not work alone. All of the nutrients are required, in varying amounts, for a well-balanced diet. The amounts needed are variable, depending upon the dog and such factors as age, general health, activity level, temperament and environment (as discussed in Chapter Two).

In this chapter, we will discuss six of the eight basic building blocks:
- water
- enzymes
- protein
- carbohydrates

• fats
• fiber

In Chapter Four, we will continue with vitamins and minerals.

WATER: THE MAGIC LIQUID

A simple substance, water is one of the most abundant and important resources of our planet and one that is taken for granted more than anything else. However, without water, life as we know it would cease to exist.

The adult dog's body is approximately two-thirds water. Blood is slightly over 80 percent water, muscles are over 70 percent water and the brain is almost 75 percent water. Even bones are 20 percent water.

Water is required for the normal functioning of every cell in the body. Respiration, digestion, metabolism and elimination all require water. Water is needed to dissolve and transport nutrients. Water keeps all things in balance; only oxygen is more necessary to preserve life.

A certain amount of water is lost each day through respiration and elimination, and must be replaced. The amount of water needed by each dog can vary depending upon the size and age of the dog, its activity level and the climate, especially the temperature.

Dehydration occurs when the dog is losing more water than it is taking in; in severe, untreated cases, it can be fatal. If water is available to them, mildly dehydrated dogs will usually drink on their own. However, moderately to severely dehydrated dogs may refuse to eat and drink; these cases need veterinary treatment and intravenous fluids immediately. *Because water is so vital, dogs should be allowed free access to clean water at all times.*

WILLARD WATER

"Willard Water" is named after its inventor, Dr. John Willard, a professor emeritus of chemistry at the South Dakota School of Mines and Technology. Dr. Willard discovered he could change the molecular structure of ordinary water, to which he then added fossilized organics from refined lignite to "reactive" it. Willard Water has been credited with aiding crop growth, destressing cattle, healing abrasions, reducing scarring and conditioning hair. Ask your health food store about ordering Willard Water, or call L&H Vitamins in Long Island City, New York, at 800-221-1152. Read more about Willard Water in the book *Aqua Vitae* (see Bibliography).

ENZYMES: THE ESSENTIAL BUILDING BLOCKS

Enzymes have numerous essential functions in the dog's body; so many, in fact, that the dog couldn't live without them. Enzymes are made up of two parts: One part is the protein molecule and the other is called the coenzyme. This coenzyme may be a vitamin, or a chemical derivative of a vitamin. Enzymes work by initiating a chemical reaction so that other substances can do their jobs.

The digesting and metabolizing of food requires a complex system of enzymes to make sure that thousands of different chemical reactions happen as they should. In the digestive process, an enzyme is capable of breaking down one specific substance. For example, an enzyme designed to break down carbohydrates does not metabolize fats, and the enzyme that breaks down milk products does not break down carbohydrates.

In dogs, the four basic digestive enzymes are: *proteases,* which break down protein; *amylases,* which break down carbohydrates; *lipases,* which break down fats; and *cellulases,* which break down vegetable matter. By "breaking down" the food, the nutrients in the food then become available for use by the body.

Because enzymes are made up of proteins and other substances, usually vitamins, the number of enzymes available for use by the dog can vary and can depend on the dog's diet. However, enzyme supplements are available and will be discussed in Chapter Seven.

PROTEIN: THE FOUNDATION FOOD

After water, protein is the most plentiful element in an animal's body, representing approximately 50 percent of each cell in the body. Proteins are incredibly diverse, serving as building blocks of hair, claws, skin, muscle, tendons, cartilage and other connective tissues. Protein is one of the most important elements of food for growth, development and repair of body tissues; sexual development; and metabolism. Proteins are also vital parts of the bloodstream, the immune system, the digestive system, hormone production and much, much more.

AMINO ACIDS. During digestion, large protein molecules are broken down by chemical action into smaller molecules to form *amino acids*. Amino acids are interesting molecules; they are both the end process of protein digestion and the molecules from which protein can be constructed.

Amino acids are vital to the transmission of nerve impulses and, as a result, are needed for muscular contractions and for the electrical impulses in the brain and spinal cord. Amino acids are involved in the formation of DNA and in the functioning of the immune system. The body's chemistry is so interwoven and so dependent upon other substances and chemicals that an imbalance of even one amino acid can throw the whole system out of kilter.

Some amino acids are produced by the body. These include *alanine, glycine, serine* and *tyrosine*. Other amino acids are not produced by the body and must be supplied by food. These essential amino acids include *arginine, histidine, leucine, lysine* and *valine*.

COMPLETE AND INCOMPLETE PROTEINS. Protein sources that contain all of the amino acids, such as lean meat, whole eggs or milk, are called *complete protein sources*. Sources of protein that do not contain a balanced amount of amino acids, such as soybeans, wheat or corn, are called *incomplete proteins*.

Besides being a major building block of your dog's body, protein can also be used as a source of heat and energy. If your body does not have enough stored fats or carbohydrates for use in times of need, protein can be metabolized in their place. In addition, excess protein not needed for body functioning or repair can be converted into fat by the liver and stored for future use.

The American Association of Feed Control Officials (AAFCO) has set guidelines for protein content in dog foods (see Chapter One, Figure 1). Reproducing or lactating dogs and growing puppies should consume a food containing no less than 22 percent protein and adult dogs should have a maintenance food containing no less than 18 percent protein.

It is important to remember that these guidelines do not take into account the digestibility of the food being consumed or the quality of the ingredients. However, they do serve as guidelines for manufacturers and consumers. (Later in this book we will discuss the quality of ingredients and how to understand dog food labels.)

Additional protein is needed for working dogs, active dogs or dogs facing stress in other ways. Dogs recuperating from injuries, illnesses or surgery also need more protein to rebuild, repair or replace worn-out tissues.

GETTING THE RIGHT AMOUNT. Too much protein is not usually a problem in young, active dogs, except that it might cause a fluid imbalance. Usually the dog's body can metabolize the excess protein and store it for future use. However, older dogs or dogs deficient in a specific amino acid might have problems with too much protein, with potentially serious results, including possible kidney failure. Therefore, excess protein is not advised—more is *not* better in this situation.

Protein deficiencies may result in growth abnormalities, especially skeletal deformities. The skin and coat may also be affected, depending upon the extent of the deficiency, with the coat appearing thin, dull and lifeless. Protein deficiency may also show up as a lack of energy and stamina, mental dullness and even depression. With protein deficiency, there will also be a notable weakness of the immune system and the dog will be open to infection and disease.

SOURCES OF PROTEIN. Dog foods supply protein from a number of different sources. Some, as discussed above, are complete proteins containing all of the essential amino acids; others are not. Along the same lines, some of the protein sources are more digestible (more usable) by the dog than others. For these and other reasons (including cost to the manufacturer and availability), most dog foods have more than one source of protein.

Beef, chicken, turkey and *lamb* are the most common sources of protein from meat. Occasionally a dog food will have fish as a protein source. A few dog food manufacturers use pork. *Meat by-products*— meat and bone meal, liver, organ meats and other meat products—are protein sources, as well as eggs, milk and milk products, including whey and cheese.

Most dogs can actually digest and metabolize about 75 percent of the meat they eat. However, many of the meat by-products are not as easily metabolized and much is wasted. Also, the high temperatures used to process the food reduce the overall protein quality.

Many different vegetable proteins are also commonly used, including wheat in various forms (whole wheat, wheat germ, wheat flour), *corn, rice, soy, barley* and other grains. Some dog foods will include *alfalfa meal, carrots, peas, beans* or *potatoes.*

CARBOHYDRATES: THE ENERGY BUILDING BLOCKS

Carbohydrates are the major element in most plants, accounting for 60 to 75 percent of the dry-matter weight of plants. Like proteins, carbohydrates have more than one use in the dog's body once eaten:

- Carbohydrates supply energy for bodily functions and are needed to assist in the digestion of other foods, especially fats.
- Carbohydrates help regulate protein and are one of the most important sources of energy for muscular exertion.

Most carbohydrates present in foods are *sugars, starches* and *cellulose.*

Sugars and *starches* are easily digested and are converted to a simple sugar, such as glucose. This is used by the body as fuel for the muscles as well as the brain and the nervous system. Excess glucose (sugar from plant material) is converted to glycogen and is stored in the liver and muscles for future use.

Cellulose is not easily digested by the dog and serves as fiber for water regulation in the large intestine, aiding in the formation and elimination of feces.

As previously discussed, proteins also supply energy to the dog's body. However, proteins have other functions that carbohydrates do not. Therefore, when there are enough carbohydrates, the body uses them to meet energy needs and proteins to serve their other functions. Too few carbohydrates, and the body will tap into protein reserves to fulfill energy demands.

The dog's carbohydrate needs depend upon many variables, including general health, activity level and energy needs. A carbohydrate deficiency may produce a loss of energy, weight loss, poor condition, depression and a breakdown of essential body protein.

SOURCES OF CARBOHYDRATES. Corn, rice, oats, potatoes and wheat are good sources of carbohydrates because they are easily digested by the dog after processing. Vegetables and other grains that supply proteins to the dog can also be a good source of carbohydrates.

FATS: THE "GOOD COAT" BUILDING BLOCK

Most dog owners have heard, somewhere, that fats are necessary for a dog to have a shiny, healthy coat. That statement is partly true; a fat deficiency will show up as dry, flaky skin. However, fats in the diet do more than create a shiny coat, and all fats are not the same.

Dietary fats, called *lipids*, are a group of compounds that are not soluble in water and have a number of different functions in the dog's body. Some lipids are part of cell structures; that others are part of the blood plasma. *Lipids serve as carriers for the fat-soluble vitamins A, D, E and K.*

Fats are also involved in many different chemical processes in the body. Fatty layers under the skin serve as an insulator against heat loss. The fatty acids are an important component of lipids. The alpha-linolenate acids are three fatty acids—oleic, linoleic and linolenic—that cannot be manufactured by the dog's body and must be supplied by food. They are necessary for normal growth; healthy blood, arteries and nerves; normal kidney function; and keeping the skin and hair coat healthy and supple.

Fats are also the primary source of energy for your dog. *Fats furnish more than twice the number of calories (or energy) per gram than do carbohydrates or protein.*

Too much fat can lead to obesity and its associated problems. Excessive fat intake will also slow down digestion, resulting in nausea, diarrhea and, sometimes, vomiting. A fat deficiency will often show up as dry, flaky skin and dull hair coat. An extreme deficiency in a young dog will lead to slow growth. A rare fatty acid deficiency may show up as liver disease, pancreatitis or chronic digestive disorders.

SOURCES OF FATS. Animal fats are one source of fat that many dog food manufacturers add to their foods, both to increase palatability and for the fat itself. However, the high temperatures used to process foods can eliminate the fatty acid content of the food and destroy part of its effectiveness to the dog.

Some dog food manufacturers add a cold-pressed oil—such as linseed, wheat germ or soybean—to supply the needed lipids. Ideally, the dog food should contain animal fat and a cold-pressed oil, and the label should list all three of the fatty acids: oleic acid, linolenic acid and linoleic acid.

The AAFCO recommends that growing puppies or pregnant or lactating bitches eat a dog food containing no less than 8 percent fat with no less than 1 percent linoleic acid. Adult dogs should have no less than 5 percent fat with, again, no less than 1 percent linoleic acid.

FIBER: THE "ACTION" BUILDING BLOCK

Fiber is the part of food that is not digested by the dog's body. Cellulose is a good example of a fiber. Just because it is not digested doesn't mean it's worthless or wasted food, though. Fiber contributes essentially to good intestinal health by absorbing water and aiding in the formation and movement of feces.

Low-calorie diets for overweight dogs normally have an increased amount of fiber because the dog can then eat a good amount of food, feel full and yet be consuming fewer calories.

BALANCING NUTRIENTS

All of these nutrients work together, as do the other building blocks mentioned in the next chapter. Even though protein is one of the most important nutrients a dog can eat, a diet of pure protein will not sustain life over a long period, and certainly will not allow for healthy reproduction.

Each individual dog has its own dietary needs for protein, fat, carbohydrates and fiber, as well as the other nutrient building blocks. The AFFCO and other guidelines are exactly that: guidelines. Guidelines for the dog food manufacturer and for the wise consumer.

HIGH AND LOW QUALITY NUTRIENT SOURCES

Ingredient	Purpose	High Quality	Low Quality
PROTEINS	To build muscles, connective tissue; influence enzyme and hormone production	chicken; poultry by-product meal; turkey by-product meal; meat meal; eggs; liver; fish; fish meal; skim milk; pork meal	meat and bone meal; feather meal
CARBO-HYDRATES	To provide starches (excellent sources of energy and fiber), promote intestinal health and for proper stool formation	corn; rice; oatmeal; oat flour; wheat	soy flour; soybean meal; corn gluten meal; wheat gluten; wheat middlings
FATS	To store energy, provide essential fatty acids and enhance palatability	poultry, chicken, turkey and pork fat. (All have low melting points and are highly digestible.)	vegetable oils; corn oil, lecithin; soy oil; wheat germ oil; sesame seed oil; linseed oil. (Secondary sources)

FIGURE 3
BUILDING BLOCK COMPARISONS:
PUPPY/GROWTH DRY FOODS

Company/Food	Protein	Fat	Fiber	Moisture
Pet Products Plus				
Excell Puppy	28	18	3.5	10
Lamb & Rice Puppy	28	15	3.5	10
Breeder's Choice Growth	28	17	4	10
Nutro Lamb & Rice Puppy	26	12	5	10
Max Puppy	28	17	4	10
Vet's Choice Select Balance				
Puppy	26	17	3	10
Kruse's Country Perfection				
Puppy	26	10	3	10
Natural Life Pet Products				
Puppy	26	15	4	10
Iams Lamb Meal & Rice				
for Puppies	26	14	4	10
Purina Puppy Chow	27	9	5	12
ONE Lamb and Rice				
for Puppies	28	16	3	12
Kal Kan Pedigree Puppy	27	10	3	12

FIGURE 4
BUILDING BLOCK COMPARISONS:
ADULT/MAINTENANCE DRY FOODS

Company/Food	Protein	Fat	Fiber	Moisture
Iams				
Mini Chunks	26	15	5	10
Eukanuba Original	30	20	4	10
Joy Special Meal	26	10	4	12
Super Pro Adult	26	15	4	11
Pet Products Plus				
Excell Mini Chunks	26	15	3.5	10
Adult Lamb & Rice	25	12	3.5	10
Vet's Choice				
Adult Lamb & Rice	26	16	5	10
Select Balance Adult	22	13	3	10
Breeder's Choice				
Maintenance	25	15	3.5	10
Lamb & Rice	23	12	3.5	10
Nature's Recipe				
Chicken Meal & Barley	25	15	4.5	10
Lamb Meal, Rice, Barley	20	10	4.5	10
Hill's Pet Nutrition				
Science Diet Maintenance	22	13	3	10
Natural Life Pet Products				
Lambaderm	22	10	4	10
Vegetarian	17.5	7.5	4.5	10
Kal Kan Pedigree				
Mealtime with Rice and Vegetables	21	8	4	12
Kruse's Country Perfection				
Adult	18	8	3	10

FIGURE 4, CON'T.

Company/Food	Protein	Fat	Fiber	Moisture
Ken L Ration				
Cycle Adult	22	8	4	10
Gravy Train Beef	21	8	4	10
Biskit	24	7	3	10
Purina				
Gravy	21	8	4.5	12
Dog Chow	21	8	4.5	12
Pro Plan Adult	25	15	3	12
Turkey and Barley	25.4	16.5	2	10.2
Nature's Course	21	10	5.5	12
Alpo Beef	21	8	4.5	12

FIGURE 5
BUILDING BLOCK COMPARISONS:
PERFORMANCE DRY FOODS

Company/Food	Protein	Fat	Fiber	Moisture
Natural Life Condition	28	18	3.5	10
Alpo Protein Plus	28	11	4	12
Nutro Natural Choice Plus	27	18	4	3
Purina				
Hi Pro	27	10	4	12
Pro Plan Performance	30	20	3	12
Super Pro Performance	27	22	14	11
Fromm Performance	26	18	3.5	10
Competition	22	15	4	10
Walthum Adult Conditioning	25	11	3	12
Kal Kan Pedigree				
Expert Conditioning	25	11	3	12

FIGURE 6
BUILDING BLOCK COMPARISONS:
REDUCING/LESS ACTIVE DRY FOODS

Company/Food	Protein	Fat	Fiber	Moisture
Iams Eukanuba Light	19	9	4	10
Pet Products Plus				
Reduced Calorie				
Chicken & Rice	18	7	5	10
Breeder's Choice Lite	17	8	7	10
Vet's Choice				
Select Balance				
Less Active	16.5	4.5	15	10
Hill's Pet Nutrition				
Science Diet Light	14	4	15	10
Purina				
Fit & Trim	14	5	10	12
Pro Plan Lite	14	8	5.5	12

FIGURE 7
BUILDING BLOCK COMPARISONS:
SENIOR/GERIATRIC DRY FOODS

Company/Food	Protein	Fat	Fiber	Moisture
Natural Life Pet Products				
Senior	18	8	4	10
Nature's Recipe Senior/Pension				
Lamb & Rice	16	8	10	10
Hill's Pet Nutrition				
Science Diet Canine Senior	16	8	4.5	10
Purina Senior	16	6.5	7	12

FIGURE 8
BUILDING BLOCK COMPARISONS:
CANNED, SEMIMOIST AND FROZEN FOODS

Company/Food	Protein	Fat	Fiber	Moisture
Quaker Oats Ken-L Ration				
King Kuts Beef (can)	8	3	1	78
Special Cuts (semimoist)	12.5	7	3	36
Kal Kan Pedigree				
Chopped Combo (can)	8	6	1.5	78
Hill's Pet Nutrition				
Science Diet Growth (can)	8	5	1	74
Maintenance (can)	7	4	1	74
Senior (can)	4.5	3.5	1.5	74
Friskies Pet Care				
Mighty Dog Senior (can)	6	4.5	1	78
Purina Moist and Meaty				
Butcher's Burgers (semimoist)	18	7	3	33
Lean (semimoist)	18	5	3	33
Walter Kendall				
Baked Loaf Dog Food (frozen)	13	6	1.25	65
Chicken Loaf (frozen)	11	7	1.25	65

FOUR

THE OTHER BUILDING BLOCKS:
VITAMINS AND MINERALS

The discovery of vitamins in 1910 was one of the most exciting achievements in the field of nutrition. Prior to their discovery, researchers knew that substances were needed for good health, but those substances were unknown. Although nutritionists and researchers have learned much about vitamins since their discovery, experts readily admit there is still much more to learn, including the amounts of many vitamins needed for good health.

For example, in 1970 Linus Pauling created havoc in the nutritional and medical fields when his experiments seemed to show that massive doses of vitamin C could prevent or cure many diseases. Research is still continuing and is constantly producing therapeutic applications for vitamins.

WHAT ARE VITAMINS AND WHAT DO THEY DO?

Vitamins are organic substances found only in plants or animals. With a few exceptions, the dog's body cannot synthesize vitamins; therefore, vitamins must be supplied in the dog's food or in supplements.

In your dog's body, vitamins function together and, with enzymes, perform a variety of different functions, including digestion, metabolism, growth, reproduction and oxidation.

Vitamins, in a nutshell, are responsible for releasing nutrients from food sources, and are required for tens of thousands of different chemical reactions. There are fat-soluble vitamins (vitamins A, D, K and E), which are stored by the body in fatty tissue and the liver, and water-soluble vitamins (vitamins B and C), which cannot be stored and are excreted daily. Because vitamins work on a cellular level, a vitamin deficiency can have a number of repercussions.

The American Association of Feed Control Officials (AAFCO) has established nutrient profiles for dog foods, including the minimum vitamin recommendations for dogs. (See Figure 1 in Chapter One for the AAFCO chart.)

SHOULD YOU SUPPLEMENT?

Deciding which vitamins your dog should get and how much of each is very difficult, even for researchers. Some researchers feel that today's commercial dog foods contain more vitamins and minerals than the AAFCO minimums and that over-supplementation can destroy the nutritional balance of the food and even be hazardous to the dog's health.

Other researchers believe that a certain amount of supplementation is needed for several reasons, the most important being that the high temperatures used for processing dog foods can affect the nutritional value of the food. Some ingredients may contain the needed vitamins, but the dog may not be able to digest and metabolize them adequately. The ability to metabolize vitamins can be affected by the quality and type of ingredients being eaten, the dog's breed heritage, age, general health and medication.

Before deciding to add vitamin supplements to your dog's diet, research the food you are feeding (or would like to feed) and find out about the quality of the ingredients. Find out also if vitamins are added to the food. Look at your dog: What is the dog's state of health? Is its coat shiny and healthy? Is the dog happy and energetic? Is it mentally alert? If you have any questions, talk to your veterinarian.

INDIVIDUAL VITAMINS, EXPLAINED

The vitamins described below are listed in alphabetical order. Figure 9 at the end of this chapter summarizes symptoms of vitamin deficiencies and excesses. Figure 10 gives you information on vitamin sources.

VITAMIN A. Vitamin A is a fat-soluble vitamin that has two forms: *preformed vitamin A* and *provitamin A*. Provitamin A is carotene, which must be converted into vitamin A before it can be used by the body. Preformed vitamin A is the result of that chemical conversion. As a fat-soluble vitamin, excess vitamin A is stored in the liver and in fat tissues, lungs, kidneys and the retinas of the eyes.

Vitamin A is an important antioxidant; it helps in growth and repair of body tissues, aids in digestion, protects mucous membranes and helps disease resistance. An immune system—enhancing substance, vitamin A is also necessary for building strong bones, teeth and claws, as well as healthy blood. Vitamin A is also responsible for good eyesight.

A vitamin A deficiency will cause slow or retarded growth, reproductive failure and skin disorders. Secondary infections are also common, as are eye disorders. Because vitamin A is a fat-soluble vitamin, if too much is ingested, it can be toxic. Too much vitamin A has also been associated with bone deformities, joint pain and bleeding.

AAFCO recommends a minimum of 5,000 International Units (IU) per day per kilogram of dry food, for puppies, gestating or lactating bitches and adult dogs, with a maximum of 50,000 IU per day.

Vitamin A can be found in green leafy vegetables, such as spinach and broccoli. It is also found in fish oils and animal liver. Most dog food manufacturers add vitamin A to the food as a supplement rather than counting on the foods to retain the vitamin during processing.

THE B VITAMINS. There are various B vitamins. This group is often called the vitamin B complex and includes B1 (thiamin), B2 (riboflavin), B3 (niacin), B5 (pantothenic acid), B6 (pyridoxine), B12 (cyanocobalamin) and B15 (pangamic acid). The B complex also includes biotin, choline, folic acid, inositol and para-aminobenzoic acid (PABA).

The B-complex vitamins help provide energy by assisting in the conversion of carbohydrates to glucose, which in turn is the body's fuel. The B vitamins also help metabolize protein and fat. These vitamins are needed for normal functioning of the nervous system, for good muscle tone and for healthy skin and hair coat.

Vitamin B1 (thiamin) works with enzymes to help convert glucose to energy. Also known as the "morale" vitamin, thiamin works with the nervous system and is beneficial to a good mental attitude. Although it is known to improve individual learning capacity in children, this has not yet been proven in dogs. The AAFCO guidelines suggest that all dogs receive no less than 1 mg/kg of thiamin daily.

Vitamin B2 (riboflavin) assists in the chemical breakdown of foods. It also works with enzymes to help cells utilize oxygen. Riboflavin is also needed for good vision and healthy skin, hair and nails. The AAFCO guidelines recommend that all dogs receive no less than 2.2 mg/kg daily.

Vitamin B3 (niacin) works with enzymes to metabolize food. It is effective in improving circulation, reducing cholesterol and maintaining a healthy nervous system. The AAFCO guidelines suggest that all dogs receive no less than 11.4 mg/kg of niacin daily.

Vitamin B5 (pantothenic acid) stimulates the adrenal glands, which increases production of adrenal hormones necessary for good health. Vitamin B5 aids digestion, is good for healthy skin and hair and also helps the body to better withstand stress. The AAFCO guidelines recommend that all dogs receive 10 mg/kg daily.

Vitamin B6 (pyridoxine) is necessary for absorption of vitamin B12. It also helps linoleic acid function better in the dog's body and is needed for the production of red blood cells and antibodies. The AAFCO guidelines suggest all dogs get 1 mg/kg daily.

Vitamin B12 (cyanocobalamin) is a cobalt-containing vitamin that works with enzymes to assist in normal DNA synthesis. B12 also works with the nervous system and food metabolism. AAFCO does not have a suggested daily dosage of cyanocobalamin, even though a deficiency can result in serious health problems, including macrocytic anemia.

Vitamin B15 (pangamic acid) works to eliminate hypoxia (oxygen insufficiency) in body tissues, especially muscles. B15 also stimulates the glandular systems. AAFCO has not established a daily requirement; however, a deficiency could cause diminished oxygenation in cells, especially in the heart.

The other B-complex vitamins also serve vital functions. *Biotin* assists in the oxidation of fatty acids and in the metabolism of other foods. Biotin is also required by the other B vitamins for metabolism.

Choline functions with inositol as a basic ingredient of lecithin. The AAFCO guidelines recommend 1,200 mg/kg of choline daily for all dogs.

Folic acid works with vitamins B12 and C to metabolize proteins. Folic acid is also necessary for the formation of red blood cells. The AAFCO guidelines suggest all dogs get 0.18 mg/kg of folic acid.

All of these B vitamins are water soluble; as a result, any excess is excreted instead of stored in the body. Because the vitamins are not retained, they must be replenished in the diet. The B-complex vitamins are found primarily in brewer's yeast, liver and whole grain cereals.

Sulfa drugs, insecticides and estrogen can destroy these vitamins in the digestive tract. It is also important to remember that most of the B vitamins work together and if given as a supplement should be given together. An excess of one B vitamin could cause a deficiency (or excess) of another.

VITAMIN C. Vitamin C (ascorbic acid) has caused more uproar than any other vitamin available. In humans, vitamin C has been labeled a "miracle" vitamin because of its supposed ability to fight the common cold. It also serves as an aid in the formation of red blood cells. Vitamin C also fights bacterial infections, maintains collagen, helps to heal wounds and prevents some hemorrhaging. Most important, vitamin C is known to help boost the immune system, fighting and killing viruses.

However, even though vitamin C has so many beneficial properties, many researchers do not think that supplementing vitamin C to dogs is needed. Dogs are able to synthesize vitamin C internally and these researchers believe that any additional vitamin C would be wasted. Some researchers also believe that excess vitamin C can cause a change in the pH balance of the kidneys.

However, many other researchers believe otherwise. Alfred Plechner, DVM, stated in his book *Pet Allergies: Remedies for an Epidemic*, "I do believe in vitamin C. It can indeed be helpful in many ways for many animals. Among other things, vitamin C contributes directly to adrenal health and function." Other experts feel vitamin C can help prevent orthopedic problems in fast-growing, large-breed dogs.

Dr. Susan Donoghue wrote in "Nutrition: Stressed Out Dogs" (*AKC Gazette*, August 1992) that certain nutrients are excreted in the urine, especially in times of stress, and vitamin C is one of those nutrients. She said, "In my research, supplementation of racing sled dogs with vitamin C appeared to lessen stress. After five months of traveling 3000 miles, sled dogs receiving vitamin C scored higher on behavior/training profiles than their partners who received a placebo."

As the debate continues, many dog food manufacturers are using ascorbic acid as a preservative. Granted, the amount used to preserve food is small, has a short shelf life and is usually mixed with other substances; however, it is a vitamin C supplement.

At this point, research (and debate) is ongoing, and until some definitive answers are found, it will be up to the individual dog owner as to whether or not to supplement vitamin C. AAFCO does not recommend amounts for vitamin C.

VITAMIN D. Known as the sunshine vitamin, vitamin D can be acquired from food or it can be absorbed from exposure to the sun. Vitamin D is needed for normal calcium-phosphorus metabolism because it aids in the absorption of calcium in the intestinal tract and the assimilation of phosphorus. Vitamin D is needed for normal growth and healthy bones and teeth.

Vitamin D works in conjunction with vitamin A, and a deficiency of either can lead to rickets and other bone diseases and deformities. It can also lead to tooth disorders, vision problems and kidney disease. Vitamin D is a fat-soluble vitamin; excess is stored in the liver, brain and skin. Too much can lead to excess calcium and phosphorus in the system, causing calcification in the blood vessels, soft tissues and kidneys.

Fish liver oils are the best sources of vitamin D, as is the sun. However, a dog with a thick double coat, like the Newfoundland, will obviously gain less benefit from sunshine than will a short-coated breed like a Labrador Retriever.

The AAFCO guidelines recommend that all dogs get a minimum of 500 IU of vitamin D daily, with a maximum of 5,000 IU per kilogram of dry dog food eaten.

VITAMIN E. Vitamin E, a fat-soluble vitamin, is actually a group of substances called *tocopherols*. Found in cold-pressed vegetable oils, raw seeds, nuts and soybeans, tocopherols are antioxidants—substances that oppose oxidation in the dog's body. Fat oxidation results in free radicals, which can cause extensive damage to the dog's body. Vitamin E protects both the pituitary and adrenal hormones from oxidation, as do the B-complex and C vitamins.

Vitamin E assists in the cellular respiration of muscle tissue, including the heart. It also dilates the blood vessels, allowing more blood to reach the heart, and it works to prevent blood clots from forming in blood vessels.

AAFCO recommends that all dogs get at least 50 IU/kg daily, but no more than 1,000 IU. A deficiency of vitamin E can result in a number of disorders, including kidney failure, heart disease, blood disorders and premature birth.

Many dog food manufacturers use tocopherols and ascorbic acids as preservatives.

VITAMIN K. Vitamin K is necessary for blood clotting and for normal liver function. Injections of vitamin K are often given to dogs with bleeding disorders, or prior to surgery to help control bleeding.

Vitamin K is fat-soluble, and toxicity and abnormal blood clotting can result from too high a dosage. However, AAFCO has not established guidelines for this vitamin.

The best sources of vitamin K are green leafy vegetables, milk, yogurt, eggs and fish oils. There are no AAFCO recommendations for vitamin K.

ALL ABOUT MINERALS

Minerals are present, to some extent, in the tissues of all living things. Minerals make up parts of your dog's bones, teeth, muscles, blood and nerves. Minerals help keep the bones strong and the nerves healthy and reactive.

Minerals work with vitamins, with enzymes and with each other. For example, calcium and phosphorus are so closely related and their functions so intertwined, they could actually be called one mineral: calcium-phosphorus. But they are really two minerals that function best together. Many other vitamins and minerals work the same way. The B-complex vitamins also need phosphorus for maximum metabolism; iron needs vitamin C for best absorption and zinc helps vitamin A to be released from the liver. A deficiency in any one mineral can have drastic effects on many systems in the body.

INDIVIDUAL MINERALS EXPLAINED

The minerals are listed alphabetically. Figure 11 at the end of this chapter lists sources of minerals; Figure 12 summarizes mineral deficiencies and excesses.

CALCIUM AND PHOSPHORUS. As was just mentioned, calcium and phosphorus are two separate minerals, but their functions are so closely intertwined they could almost be referred to as one combined mineral.

Calcium is needed for muscle contraction and neuromuscular transmission and for blood coagulation. Calcium is also vital to some of the body's enzyme reactions.

Because it is present in every cell, phosphorus plays a part in nearly all chemical reactions in the body. It is part of the digestive process, and in the production of energy it helps stimulate muscle contractions, including that of the heart muscle. Phosphorus plays a vital part in cell reproduction. Working together, calcium's and phosphorus's most important function is to strengthen bones and teeth.

A calcium deficiency can cause rickets and bone and skeletal disorders and malformations. Moderate deficiencies may cause muscular cramps, joint pain, slow pulse and impaired growth. Deficiencies are rare, however. What is more common is a calcium-phosphorus imbalance. Many researchers feel that calcium and phosphorus work best with a balance of 1.5 parts calcium to 1 part phosphorus, although AAFCO recommends a minimum balance of 1:1, with a maximum balance of 2:1.

Meat contains good quantities of phosphorus, while milk and milk products have both phosphorus and calcium. Many commercial dog foods have among their ingredients bone meal or calcium carbonate, either of which is a good source of these nutrients.

CHLORIDE. Chloride is found throughout the body and helps regulate the correct balance of acid and alkali in the blood. Working with salts, chloride maintains the pressure in the cells that allows fluids to pass in and out of cell membranes. It is also needed by the liver to filter wastes from the system.

A deficiency is usually rare, as chloride is found in table salt and most diets contain adequate amounts of salt. However, a deficiency of chloride can cause impaired digestion, poor muscular contraction and hair loss.

AAFCO recommends that puppies and dogs involved in a breeding program eat dog food containing no less than 0.45 percent chloride per day. Adult dogs on a maintenance diet should get no less than 0.09 percent, with no maximum amount specified.

COPPER. Copper assists in the absorption of iron, which is required for hemoglobin synthesis. Copper is also involved in the healing process and helps oxidize vitamin C. Copper is needed to build strong bones, to synthesize phospholipids and to form elastin.

A copper deficiency results in a type of anemia much like that caused by an iron deficiency. A deficiency can also cause bone or skeletal abnormalities. Bedlington Terriers, for example, have a genetic problem that interferes with the process of metabolizing copper, causing a predisposition to hepatitis. Doberman Pinschers also have a genetic disorder associated with the metabolization of copper.

Copper is found in liver and fish, as well as whole grains and legumes. The amount of copper found in plant sources can vary depending upon the richness of the mineral in the soil where they were grown.

AAFCO recommends that all dogs should get a minimum of 7.3 mg of copper per kilogram of dry food daily, with a maximum of 250 mg/kg.

IODINE. Iodine is a trace mineral that is vital to the proper functioning of the thyroid gland. It plays an important part in regulating the body's energy, in promoting growth and in stimulating the rate of metabolism.

Iodine is found in fish, as well as iodized salt (salt with iodine added). Many commercial dog foods add iodine or potassium iodide as a supplement.

AAFCO recommends that all dogs get 1.5 mg/kg daily, with a maximum of 50 mg/kg. A deficiency can cause hypothyroidism (an abnormally low secretion of the thyroid hormones), obesity, sluggishness, dry hair, nervousness and irritability.

IRON. Iron, working with protein, is present in every living cell in the body. The primary function of iron is to combine with protein and copper to make hemoglobin, which transports oxygen. Iron also works with enzymes to promote protein metabolism. Besides proteins and copper, iron needs calcium to work properly.

Iron is found in liver, lean meats and fish. Leafy green vegetables, whole grains and legumes also contain iron.

The AAFCO guidelines suggest that all dogs get at least 80 mg/kg of iron daily, with a maximum of 3,000 mg/kg. A deficiency of iron can cause anemia, symptoms of which can include difficulty breathing and constipation.

MAGNESIUM. Magnesium helps promote the absorption and metabolism of vitamins and other minerals, including vitamins C and E, calcium, phosphorus, sodium and potassium. Magnesium is also important to protein and carbohydrate metabolism. It aids bone growth;

in fact, over 70 percent of all magnesium is located in the bones.

Magnesium can be found in leafy green vegetables, raw wheat germ and other whole grains, soybeans, milk, fish and oil-rich nuts and seeds. It is important to keep in mind that cooking, especially at high temperatures, removes magnesium from food.

AAFCO recommends that dog food contain at least 0.04 percent magnesium, with no more than 0.3 percent. A deficiency will cause cardiac irregularities, muscle twitch and tremors and depression.

ZINC. Zinc is a trace element with a number of important functions. It is vital in the metabolism of various vitamins, including the B-complex vitamins. Zinc is also a part of many different enzymes necessary for digestion and metabolism, and it promotes healing.

Too much calcium in the diet can hamper the absorption of zinc, as can a diet too high in cellulose. A deficiency will show up as delayed sexual maturity, slow or retarded growth or diabetes. Skin problems are common in dogs not getting enough zinc. AAFCO recommends that all dogs eat a dog food containing a minimum of 120 mg per kilogram of dry matter, with a maximum of 1,000 mg/kg.

OTHER MINERALS. There are several other minerals important to your dog's good health. Selenium works with an enzyme and vitamin E to protect cells. Selenium is found in both meats and cereals, and a deficiency is rare. Manganese, too, works with enzymes and is important to bone growth and reproduction. (See Figures 11 and 12.)

MAINTAINING A BALANCE

When discussing your dog's vitamin and mineral needs, it's important to keep in mind that no single vitamin or mineral functions alone; each has its own function and place in the system, but each is also dependent upon the others. Even if you or your veterinarian decides that your dog has a deficiency, you must remember to keep the balance of all the nutrients when you supplement your dog's diet.

Chapter Eight will elaborate on the issue of supplements, so keep reading.

FIGURE 9
VITAMIN DEFICIENCIES AND EXCESSES

Vitamin A

Deficiency: Vision problems, slow growth, skin and coat problems, diarrhea.

Excess: Nausea, vomiting, diarrhea, hair loss, bone deformities, bleeding disorders.

Vitamin B Complex

Deficiency: Fatigue, irritability, nervousness, hair loss, skin problems.

Excess: Water soluble; when taken as a complex, excess is usually excreted in the urine. Unusual excess can cause nerve damage, blood or digestive disorders.

Vitamin C (Research ongoing and greatly debated)

Deficiency: Impaired lactation, shortness of breath, swollen joints, slow healing, poor dental condition.

Excess: Water soluble; most excess excreted in the urine. High doses can result in diarrhea.

Vitamin D

Deficiency: Rickets, bone deformities, poorly developed muscles, nervous disorders, vision problems.

Excess: Increased frequency of urination, nausea, vomiting, muscular weakness, calcification of muscles, including the heart.

Vitamin E

Deficiency: Blood and bleeding disorders, collagen problems, amino acid breakdown, reduction in functioning of several hormones, reproductive failure.

Excess: Generally considered nontoxic; however, can cause elevated blood pressure.

Vitamin K

Deficiency: Bleeding disorders, miscarriage.

Excess: Generally considered nontoxic.

FIGURE 10
SOURCES OF VITAMINS

Vitamin	Most Common Source
Vitamin A	Dairy products, leafy green vegetables, fish liver oil, carrots.
Vitamin B Complex	Brewer's yeast, whole grain cereals, liver.
Vitamin C	Fruits and vegetables, especially broccoli, cabbage, leafy green vegetables.
Vitamin D	Sunshine, dairy products, fish liver oil.
Vitamin E	Cold-pressed vegetable oil, meats, raw nuts and seeds, leafy green vegetables, soybeans.
Vitamin K	Kelp, alfalfa, yogurt, egg yolk, fish liver oils.

FIGURE 11
SOURCES OF MINERALS

Mineral	Most Common Source
Calcium	Meats, bone and bone meal, milk and milk products
Chloride	Salt (sodium chloride), kelp
Copper	Liver, whole grain products, leafy green vegetables, legumes
Iodine	Fish, kelp
Iron	Liver, oysters, fish, lean meats, leafy green vegetables, whole grains, legumes, molasses
Magnesium	Green vegetables, raw whole grains, oil-rich seeds and nuts, soybeans, milk
Manganese	Whole grains, eggs, seeds and nuts, green vegetables
Phosphorus	Meat, fish, poultry, eggs, whole grains, seeds and nuts
Potassium	All vegetables, potatoes, bananas, whole grains, sunflower seeds
Selenium	Yeast, organ and muscle meats, fish, whole grains
Sulfur	Eggs, meat, cheese
Zinc	Whole grains, brewer's yeast, wheat germ, pumpkin seeds

FIGURE 12
MINERAL DEFICIENCIES AND EXCESSES

Calcium/Phosphorus
Deficiency: Rickets, bone deformities, slow growth, irritability,
   depression.
Excess: Must have balance between both minerals.

Chloride
Deficiency: Hair loss, impaired digestion, poor muscular contraction.
Excess: Adverse reactions suspected but unknown.

Copper
Deficiency: General weakness, impaired respiration, anemia, skeletal
   abnormalities, skin sores.
Excess: Toxic hepatitis.

Iodine
Deficiency: Enlarged thyroid, dry skin and hair coat, loss of vigor,
   slow/poor growth, reproductive failure.
Excess: Unknown.

Iron
Deficiency: Weakness, constipation, anemia.
Excess: Unknown.

Magnesium
Deficiency: Neuromuscular excitability or irritability, tremors,
   depression.
Excess: Unknown.

Manganese
Deficiency: Slow or retarded growth, reproductive failure, abnormal
   bone growth, paralysis, ataxia, blindness, deafness.
Excess: Unknown.

Potassium
Deficiency: Respiratory failure, cardiac arrest, nervous disorders,
   insomnia.
Excess: Unknown.

Selenium
Deficiency: Premature aging, puppy death, skeletal and cardiac
    myopathies.
Excess: Hepatitis, nephritis.

Sulfur
Deficiency: Slow or retarded growth, sluggishness, fatigue.
Excess: Unknown.

Zinc
Deficiency: Retarded growth, delayed sexual maturity, diabetes, skin
    problems.
Excess: Relatively nontoxic, but excessive intake may have harmful side
    effects.

FIVE

UNDERSTANDING DOG FOOD AND DOG FOOD LABELS

In previous chapters we discussed your dog's nutritional needs: proteins for energy, for building healthy cells and for growth; fats for processing vitamins and keeping skin and coat healthy; carbohydrates and fiber for energy and digestibility and, of course, plenty of clean water. We know that vitamins and minerals often work with each other and with enzymes for cell function and growth. We even know what foods contain these nutritional building blocks. But how do we know whether a commercial food is supplying these needs?

Unfortunately, there is no easy answer. In fact, the nutritional needs of dogs and the quality of commercial dog foods are two highly debated subjects—ones that have some researchers fervently defending one position and others arguing exactly the opposite.

Alfred Plechner, DVM, author of *Pet Allergies: Remedies for an Epidemic* (Very Healthy Enterprises, 1986), states in his book, "I discovered that many commercial food formulations are woefully deficient in key nutrients." He continues by condemning the quality of the ingredients used by many dog food manufacturers—the moldy grains, rancid foods and meat meal made from slaughterhouse discards.

However, the dog food companies emphasize the quality of their foods and point to the generations of dogs residing in their care centers, eating the food the company produces and looking the picture of health.

In this chapter, we will discuss both sides of the various issues as thoroughly as possible. Ultimately, it's up to you as the dog owner and consumer to decide what you want your dog to eat.

DISSECTING THE DOG FOOD LABEL

Every dog food label must include specific information, which is usually divided into two parts: the principal display panel and the information panel.

The **principal display panel** is very straightforward. It provides the food's

1. brand name (Iams, Purina, Kal-Kan, etc.)
2. identity statement (describes the contents: "Beef Dinner," "Lamb and Rice," etc.)
3. designator (identifies species and growth stage for which food is intended: "for dogs," "for puppies," etc.)
4. quantity of contents (identifies weight of contents)

The **information panel** provides the food's

1. guaranteed analysis (shows the "as is" percentages of food's constituents)
2. ingredient list (shows ingredients in descending order, by weight)
3. nutritional adequacy claim (identifies specific life stage for which food is intended and whether animal feeding tests based on AAFCO procedures were used)
4. feeding instructions (how much of the food to give your dog)

The principal display panel is like the name of your town: It identifies where you are, but it doesn't tell you how to get around. For a "road map" of the food, you need to be able to "read" the stuff on the information panel. Let's review the first three items found there.

GUARANTEED ANALYSIS

The guaranteed analysis on the information panel of the dog food label lists the minimum levels of crude protein and fat and the maximum levels of fiber and water. "Crude" refers to the total protein content, not necessarily the amount of protein that is actually digestible. Therefore, the crude protein and fat amounts are simply rough guides. The actual amount depends upon the ingredients and their quality.

4 Legged FOODS

BOW-WOW CHOW BEEF FORMULA

GUARANTEED ANALYSIS

Crude Protein (Minimum)............................21%
Crude Fat (Minimum)...............................12%
Linoleic Acid (Minimum)...........................4.5%
Crude Fiber (Maximum)............................5%
Moisture (Maximum)..............................10%
Vitamin E (Minimum)...........................100 IU/kg

INGREDIENTS

Beef, Meat Meal, Bone Meal, Sunflower Oil (Preserved with mixed Tocopherols, a Source of Natural Vitamin E and Ascorbic Acid), Dried Whole Egg, Natural Flavors, Monosodium Phosphate, Dried Kelp (Source of Iodine), Choline Chloride, Vitamin E Supplement, Zinc Sulfate, Ascorbic Acid (Source of Vitamin C), Niacin, Ferrous Sulfate, Calcium Pantothenate, Vitamin A Supplement, Manganous Oxide, Thiamine Mononitrate (Source of Vitamin E1), Vitamin D3 Supplement, Riboflavin Supplement (Source of Vitamin B2), Vitamin B12 Supplement, Pyridoxine Hydrochloride (Source of Vitamin B5), Inositol, Folic Acid, Cobalt Carbonate, Biotin.

SATISFACTION 100% GUARANTEED

4-Legged Food's **BOW-WOW CHOW** provides complete and balanced nutrition for all stages of a dog's life substantiated by feeding tests performed in accordance with the procedures established by the Association of American Feed Control Officials (AAFCO).

FEEDING GUIDELINES

4-Legged Food's **BOW-WOW CHOW** is a high quality, high performance dog food.
Serve dry or moistened. 4-Legged Food's **BOW-WOW CHOW** is nutritionally complete and balanced, so there is no need to add vitamins or minerals unless prescribed by a veterinarian.

Weight of Dog	Amount to Feed*
3 - 12 lbs.	1/3 - 1 1/5 cups
13 - 20 lbs.	1 1/5 - 1 3/4 cups
21 - 50 lbs.	1 3/4 - 3 1/4 cups
51 - 100 lbs.	3 1/4 - 5 cups

*Use a standard 8 oz. measuring cup.

NOTE: These are suggested amounts. Quantity will vary depending on your dog's age, environment, tempera hment, and activity.
Keep fresh drinking water available at all times. See your veterinarian regularly.

Manufactured by
4-Legged Foods, Inc.
123 Main St.
Anywhere, USA 12345
1-800-111-2222

BOW-WOW CHOW

BEEF FORMULA

• DOG FOOD •

NET WEIGHT
5LBS
(2.27kg)

A sample dog food label for packaged dry food. The left side is the principal display panel, the right is the information panel.

The amount of moisture in a food is important, especially when you are comparing foods. A food containing 24 percent protein and 10 percent moisture would have less protein per serving than a food with the same percentage of protein listed on the label but only 6 percent moisture. This is why the AAFCO guidelines (Chapter One, Figure 1) are formulated on a dry matter basis, so that all foods can be compared equally. Figure 13 has a conversion formula so you can find the dry matter basis of a food and then discover the actual protein or fat content of that dry matter.

The guaranteed analysis is only a starting place to read when looking at the label because it contains so little information. Hill's Pet Products, makers of Science Diet foods, used an advertisement in 1984 that was an excellent demonstration of how the guaranteed analysis could fool the unsuspecting dog food buyer. The ad listed a guaranteed analysis, just like one from a can of dog food, and listed crude protein at 10 percent, fat at 6.5 percent, fiber at 2.4 percent and moisture at 68 percent—typical numbers for those nutrients. However, the list of ingredients was a shocker! Four pairs of old leather work shoes, one gallon of used crankcase oil, one pail of crushed coal and sixty-eight pounds of water, when analyzed, would equal the guaranteed analysis. Not very nourishing for the dog!

INGREDIENT LIST

Ingredients are listed in descending order, by weight. However, the listings may be misleading. Suppose beef is listed as the first ingredient, causing you to think it is the primary ingredient. Look again. If it's followed by wheat flour, wheat germ, wheat middlings and so on, the combined wheat products may very well total much more than the beef.

The following is a list of some of the ingredients found in commercial dog foods. These descriptions are based on the definitions for animal feed established by the Association of American Feed Control Officials (AAFCO).

MEAT OR MEAT-BASED INGREDIENTS

Meat is the clean flesh of slaughtered cattle, swine, sheep or goats. The flesh can include striated skeletal muscle, tongue, diaphragm, heart or esophagus, overlying fat and the portions of skin, sinew, nerves and blood vessels normally found with that flesh.

Meat By-Products are clean parts of slaughtered animals, not including meat. These include lungs, spleen, kidneys, brain, liver, blood, bone, partially defatted low-temperature fatty tissue, and stomach and intestines freed of their contents. It does not include hair, horns, teeth or hooves.

Meat Meal is rendered meal made from animal tissues. It cannot contain blood, hair, hoof, horn, hide trimmings, manure or stomach or rumen (the first stomach) contents, except for amounts that may be unavoidably included during processing. It cannot contain any added extraneous materials, and may not contain any more than 14 percent indigestible materials. Also, no more than 11 percent of the crude protein in the meal can be ingredients the dog cannot digest.

Meat and Bone Meal is rendered from meat, including bone, but doesn't include blood, hair, hoof, horn, hide trimmings, manure or stomach and rumen contents, except for small amounts unavoidably included during processing. It does not include any extraneous materials. Like meat meal, only 14 percent of it may be indigestible residue, and no more than 11 percent of the crude protein may be indigestible.

Poultry By-Products are clean parts of slaughtered poultry, such as heads, feet and internal organs (like heart, lungs, liver, kidneys, abdomen, intestines) and must not contain feces or foreign matter except in unavoidable trace amounts.

Poultry By-Product Meal consists of ground, rendered, clean parts of slaughtered poultry, such as necks, feet, undeveloped eggs and intestines. It does not contain feathers, except those which are unavoidably included during processing.

Dehydrated Eggs are whole dried poultry eggs.

Animal By-Product Meal is made by rendering animal tissues which don't fit any of the other ingredient categories. It still cannot contain extra hair, hoof, horn, hide trimmings, manure or stomach or rumen contents, nor any extraneous material.

Animal Digest is a powder or liquid made by taking clean, undecomposed animal tissue and breaking it down using chemical and/or enzymatic hydrolysis. Animal digest does not contain hair, horn, teeth, hooves or feathers, except in unavoidable trace amounts. Digest names must be descriptive of their contents: chicken digest must be made from chicken, beef from beef, and so on.

Beef Tallow is fat derived from beef.

Fish Meal is the clean, dried, ground tissue of undecomposed whole fish or fish cuttings, with or without the oil extracted.

Plant and Other Ingredients

Alfalfa Meal is the finely ground product of the alfalfa plant.

Dried Whey—Whey is the thin part of milk separated from the curd, or thicker part, when milk coagulates. Dried whey is this milk part, dried, and is not less than 11 percent protein or less than 61 percent lactose.

Barley is at least 80 percent good-quality barley, no more than 3 percent heat-damaged kernels, 6 percent foreign material, 20 percent other grains or 10 percent wild oats.

Barley Flour is the soft, finely ground barley meal obtained from the milling of barley.

Beet Pulp is the dried residue from production of sugar from sugar beets.

Ground Corn (also called *corn meal* or *corn chop*) is the entire corn kernel ground or chopped. It must contain no more than 4 percent foreign material.

Corn Gluten Meal is the by-product after the manufacture of corn syrup or starch, and is the dried residue after the removal of the bran, germ and starch.

Brewer's Rice is small fragments of rice kernels that have been separated from larger kernels of milled rice.

Brown Rice is the unpolished rice left over after the kernels have been removed.

Soybean Meal is a by-product of the production of soybean oil.

Ground Grain Sorghum is made by grinding grains of sorghum.

Cereal Food Fines is a by-product of breakfast cereal production, and consists of particles of the foods.

Linseed Meal is the residue of flaxseed oil production, ground into a meal.

Peanut Hulls are the ground outer hull of the peanut shell.

Dried Kelp is dried seaweed. The maximum percentage of salt and minimum percentage of potassium and iodine must be declared.

Preservatives

BHA and BHT are both preservatives. BHA is *butylated hydroxyanisole*. BHT is *butylated hydroxytoluene*. According to Dr. Plechner, both have been associated with liver damage, fetal abnormalities and metabolic stress, and have, as Dr. Plechner states, "a questionable relationship to cancer."

Ethoxyquin has been the most highly debated item in dog foods for the last several years. Ethoxyquin is a chemical preservative that has been widely used to prevent spoilage in dog foods. Ethoxyquin was approved by the FDA in 1956. It has been alleged that ethoxyquin has caused cancer; liver, kidney and thyroid dysfunctions; reproductive failure and more, though the allegations have not been proven in tests to date.

An independent testing laboratory is conducting a new test on ethoxyquin. This test is following testing protocols approved by the US Food and Drug Administration. The FDA will evaluate the study prior to the results being released to the public.

Many dog food manufacturers still use ethoxyquin (see Figure 16); however, because of public concern many manufacturers have switched to other means of preserving their foods.

Sodium Nitrate is used both as a food coloring (red) and as a preservative. When used in food, sodium nitrate can produce carcinogenic substances called nitrosamines. Accidental ingestion of sodium nitrate by people can be fatal.

Tocopherols (vitamins C and E) are naturally occurring compounds used as natural preservatives. Tocopherols function as antioxidants, preventing the oxidation of fatty acids, vitamins and some other nutrients. These are being used more frequently as preservatives, as many dog owners are more concerned about chemical preservatives. Tocopherols have a very short shelf life, especially once the bag of food has been opened.

WHAT ARE THOSE OTHER INGREDIENTS?

The National Research Council believes that adequate amounts of needed nutrients can be obtained by eating a well-balanced diet consisting of a selection of proper ingredients. However, Lavon J. Dunne, author of the *Nutrition Almanac* (McGraw Hill, 1990) states that there is much more to nutrition than that. "Other factors affecting adequate nutrition are insufficient soil nutrient levels resulting in nutrient-deficient foods. Food processing and storage deplete foodstuffs of valuable vitamins and minerals." Dunne continues by saying that many nutrients are lost or depleted during cooking, especially at high temperatures.

When the label on dog food states that the food is complete and balanced, that means that the food contains all of the nutrients required by the Association of American Feed Control Officials (AAFCO). To satisfy these requirements, many dog food manufacturers add vitamins and minerals to the food during processing. Sometimes these are added in a natural form, as an ingredient. For example, yeast is added to many foods because it is an excellent source of selenium, chromium, iron, magnesium, manganese and other needed nutrients.

Natural vitamins can be separated from their original source, either plant or animal, and used as additives. The vitamin (or mineral) is considered natural as long as there has been no change to the basic molecular structure.

The vitamins and minerals can also be added in a synthetic, manufactured, form. Synthetic vitamins and minerals usually contain a salt, such as sulfate, nitrate or chloride, which helps stabilize the nutrient. Most researchers feel that the body absorbs synthetic vitamins as well as natural, with little difference in metabolism, except for vitamin E, which works much better in natural form.

Many of the chemical names listed on the dog food labels are the chemical names of natural or synthetic vitamins and minerals added to the food during processing to ensure that the food meets AAFCO requirements.

Ascorbic acid is a synthetic form of vitamin C.

Biotin is a natural B-complex vitamin.

Calcium carbonate is a natural form of calcium often used as a calcium supplement.

Calcium oxide is a natural form of calcium.

Calcium pantothenate is a high potency, synthetic source of vitamin B5.

Calcium phosphate is a calcium salt found in or derived from bones or bone meal.

Chloride or *chlorine* is an essential mineral, usually found in compound form with sodium or potassium.

Choline is a B vitamin found in eggs, liver and soy.

Choline chloride is a high potency, synthetic source of choline.

Cobalt is a trace element, an essential mineral and an integral part of vitamin B12.

Copper is a trace element, an essential mineral that can be toxic in excess.

Copper carbonate is a natural form of the mineral copper.

Copper gluconate is a synthetic form of copper.

Copper sulfate is a synthetic source of copper.

Ferrous sulfate is a synthetic, high potency source of iron.

Folic acid is a B vitamin found in yeast or liver.

Inositol is a B-complex vitamin.

Iron oxide is a natural source of iron.

Magnesium oxide is a natural source of magnesium.

Menadione sodium bisulfite complex is a source for vitamin K activity.

Pangamic acid is vitamin B15.

Pantothenic acid is vitamin B5, a coenzyme.

Potassium chloride is a high potency, synthetic source of potassium.

Potassium citrate is a natural form of potassium.

Pyridoxine hydrochloride is a synthetic source of vitamin B6.

Riboflavin is a synthetic source of vitamin B2.

Selenium is an essential mineral.

Sodium chloride is a synthetic form of salt; table salt.

Sodium selenite is a synthetic form of the essential mineral, selenium.

Thiamine hydrochloride is a synthetic source of vitamin B1, thiamine.

Thiamine mononitrate is a synthetic source of vitamin B1.

Zinc carbonate is a source of the mineral zinc.

Zinc oxide is a natural form of the mineral zinc.

Zinc sulfate is a synthetic form of the mineral zinc.

ARTIFICIAL COLORING

Many of the artificial colorings used in dog foods have been associated with potential problems. FD&C Red No. 40 is a possible carcinogen, but is widely used to keep meat looking fresh. Blue No. 2 is thought to increase dogs' sensitivity to viruses. Another color that is commonly used but has not been fully tested is Yellow No. 5. Red No. 2 and Violet No. 1 were banned by the FDA in the mid-seventies as possible carcinogens but prior to that were widely used in pet foods.

Interestingly enough, the food colorings are not for the dogs. Dogs don't care what color the food is. Food colorings are used to satisfy the dog's owner—you, the consumer.

THERE'S MORE!

Sugar is not an ingredient most people would expect to find in dog food, but many dog foods do contain sugar, especially the semimoist brands. In fact, some semimoist foods contain as much as 15 percent sugar. The sugar adds palatability and moisture, and aids in bacterial contamination prevention. Dogs do not need this amount of sugar, which can stress the pancreas and adrenal glands, causing diabetes. Completely devoid of protein, vitamins and minerals, sugar is, literally, empty calories.

Salt is added to many foods as a meat preservative. Too much salt can irritate the digestive system and can cause a mineral imbalance because the salt itself can upset the calcium/potassium balance.

REMEMBER *QUALITY*

The presence of some or all of the above-listed ingredients, which are the most commonly used dog food ingredients, or an assortment of these ingredients, doesn't necessarily mean that your dog is going to be well nourished. The ingredients must be in the right combinations and of good quality, both before and after processing.

BIOLOGICAL VALUE. The biological values of the ingredients are a key to good nutrition. The biological value of a food is the measurement of the amino acid completeness of the proteins contained by the food. Eggs are considered a wonderful source of protein because they contain all of the essential amino acids. Therefore, eggs have a biological value of 100 percent. Fish meal is 92 percent; beef is 78 percent, as is milk; wheat is 60 percent, wheat gluten 40; corn is 54 percent. Neither wheat nor corn would be an adequate diet alone, but fed together with one or two meat-based proteins capable of supplying the missing amino acids, they could supply an adequate diet.

For example, Dick Van Patten's Natural Balance Dog Food lists as its primary ingredients chicken meal, wheat flour, lamb meal, poultry fat, ground whole wheat and ground oats. These, along with the other ingredients, supply diverse protein sources, both meat- and cereal-based, which makes the biological value of the food high.

DIGESTIBILITY OF FOOD. Digestibility refers to the quantity of the food that is actually absorbed by the dog's system. The more food that is fully metabolized, the higher the digestibility figure. During feeding trials, the dogs' feces are collected and analyzed to determine the undigested residues of the food eaten. Dr. Steve Hannah, a nutrition scientist with Purina, said, "Digestibility is determined by the amount of food consumed by the dog, minus the amount of undigested or unabsorbed food in the stool." High digestibility indicates that the nutrients within a given food are available to be used by the dogs.

QUALITY BEFORE PROCESSING. Understanding the definition of an ingredient is not enough. A short description doesn't tell us exactly how good that ingredient is. Many grains grown in poor soil will lack needed vitamins and minerals; unfortunately, this is a common occurrence in the United States. Grains and vegetables can be polluted with fertilizer residues and pesticides of various kinds.

Ingredients can also be soiled with mold, mildew and fungus. The quality of meat can also be suspect. We all have stories of finding bits of hair and other unsavory additives in our hamburger—the quality of meats used for dog foods is much lower. The U.S. Department of Agriculture (USDA) has said that there is no mandatory federal inspection of ingredients used in pet food manufacturing. However, some states do inspect manufacturing plants, especially those producing canned pet foods.

In the majority of states it is legal (and common practice) for pet food manufacturers to use what are known as "4-D" meat sources: animals that are dead, dying, diseased or disabled when they arrive at the slaughterhouse. Dr. P. F. McGargle, a veterinarian and a former federal meat inspector, believes that feeding slaughterhouse wastes to pet animals increases their chances of getting cancer and other degenerative diseases. He said, "Those wastes include moldy, rancid or spoiled processed meats, as well as tissues too severely riddled with cancer to be eaten by people."

Richard H. Pitcairn, DVM, Ph.D., and Susan Hubble Pitcairn, authors of *Dr. Pitcairn's Complete Guide to Natural Health for Dogs and Cats* (1982), remind us of another group of additives that has been left off the dog food packages: hormones, insecticides and other chemicals. The majority of livestock used for food production are loaded with growth hormones, pesticides, antibiotics and other chemicals. Meat from fetal tissues of pregnant cows is naturally high in hormones, and high cooking temperatures do not get rid of them.

Dr. Steve Kritsick, a veterinarian specializing in nutrition, said in his *AKC Gazette* column, "Nutrition and Health: You Get What You Pay For" (November 1985), that although the biggest difference between price brand (supermarket), generic and major brand pet foods to most consumers is price, it is not the most important difference. The most important difference is nutrition. "The adage 'You get what you pay for' is all too true with pet food. Because consumers cannot look at the label and know whether or not a product is safe, animal lovers should consider the reputation of the manufacturer and the recommendation of their veterinarian."

WHAT DO THE DOG FOOD COMPANIES SAY?

While researching this book, I called several major dog food manufacturers, including the makers of most of the top-sellers, to ask them about this issue. In each instance I was not able to immediately speak to someone other than a receptionist so I left a message; the same message was left with all of the companies contacted. I started with my name and phone number, an introduction and what my research was for. The questions I asked were:

1. Many experts seem to feel that there are many instances of poor quality or tainted ingredients being used in dog foods. How is a

consumer to know what the quality of the food is that he or she is buying? Is price the only way to tell? Does the consumer really get what he or she pays for?

2. What are the differences between the food you are manufacturing and other foods on the market, in regards to the quality of ingredients?

3. Where do the ingredients for your foods come from and what quality control is used for those ingredients?

The responses to these questions caught me totally unaware: There was absolutely no response. Not one of the companies that I contacted returned my calls. Now, when I decided upon these questions, I knew that they were quite pointed and might be uncomfortable for some of the companies; however, by leaving a message and allowing the spokespeople time to think about the questions and perhaps research the answers, I was sure that I would at least get a response.

I may be off base, but to me, as a consumer who buys quite a bit of dog food each month, the total lack of response bothered me. I understand that perhaps the spokespeople didn't know the answers. Or if the companies buy ingredients in bulk from grain brokers, perhaps there is no way to know what some of the answers are; in that case, an "I don't know the answer" would have been appropriate. Unfortunately, the total lack of response said to me that the dog food companies I contacted didn't want to answer these questions at all.

QUALITY AFTER PROCESSING. Many nutrients—especially enzymes and some vitamins and minerals—can be damaged by the high temperatures used in processing dog foods. If the nutrients are in the raw food but are damaged during processing, they're obviously not going to help your dog.

NUTRITIONAL ADEQUACY CLAIM

Some experts take issue with the claim some dog food manufacturers make that their food is "100 percent nutritionally complete for all life stages." In John Cargill's article "Feed That Dog! Part III" (*Dog World* magazine, Sept. 1993), Dr. Randy Wysong said, "Thus, that which is absurd in human nutrition has become commonplace, expected and even mandated in pet nutrition." He continued by saying that the "100 percent complete" concept ignores the fact that each dog is an individual, with individual needs. He also said, "We don't have complete knowledge of what nutrition a pet requires." He went on to discuss other unknowns, including what damage processing causes to ingredients and what the dog actually digests from its food.

NAME, ADDRESS AND PHONE NUMBER
OF THE MANUFACTURER

This is provided so that if you have any questions or problems with the product, you can call to ask about them.

IN CLOSING

Dog foods labels do provide quite a bit of information; learning how to decipher them can take some time. However, the time to do that is not when you're standing in the aisle looking at all the foods available. Instead, study the labels at home. Most dog foods manufacturers provide pet stores and veterinarians with boxes of dog food samples; these are yours for the asking. If you get a variety of samples from different companies, you can then study those labels at home, at your leisure.

As you study, keep in mind that there is also much information not freely given on the label, such as the quality of the ingredients used. As we know, that information can be difficult to come by and you may need to rely upon the recommendation of experts, including your veterinarian, the philosophy and reputation of the company and the price of the food itself.

FIGURE 13
DRY MATTER BASIS CONVERSION

The labels of dry, canned, frozen or semimoist foods look very much alike until you get to the guaranteed analysis, which looks different. The dry food will probably have a protein percentage of between 20 and 26, while canned foods have protein percentages of about 6 to 8. Why are they so different? Primarily because of the moisture content, which will be about 65 to 80 percent for canned food and 3 to 10 percent for dry.

To compare the foods and get a good idea of what they really are, you must remove the moisture from the guaranteed analysis and compare both foods as dry matter.

This dry matter basis is also what the AAFCO uses when recommending nutritional levels for dog foods. (See Chapter One, Figure 1.)

For Dry Food

Brand X Dry Food:	Guaranteed Analysis
Protein	20%
Fat	10%
Fiber	10%
Moisture	10%

If a dry food shows that the moisture level is 10 percent, that means the dry solid matter in the food is 90 percent. To find the protein level of this dry matter, divide the 20 percent protein (from the label) by 90 percent dry solids. The answer, 22 percent, is the percentage of protein in the actual dry food.

For Canned Food

Brand Z Canned Food:	Guaranteed Analysis
Protein	5%
Fat	5%
Fiber•	10%
Moisture	80%

The conversion for canned food is the same. If the moisture level is 80 percent, that means the dry solids in this food are 20 percent. To find the protein levels of this food, the 5 percent protein (from the label) is divided by the 20 percent dry solids. The answer, 25 percent, is the protein level of the dry solid-matter food.

The fat levels of a particular food can be figured using the same formula, substituting the fat percentage from the label.

FIGURE 14
FIRST FIVE INGREDIENTS:
POPULAR DRY FOODS

Company	Food	Ingredients
Breeder's Choice	Lamb & Rice	1. lamb meal 2. brewer's rice 3. brown rice 4. beet pulp 5. poultry fat
	Growth	1. chicken meal 2. brewer's rice 3. corn 4. lamb meal 5. wheat
Dick Van Patten's	Natural Balance	1. chicken meal 2. wheat flour 3. lamb meal 4. poultry fat 5. ground whole wheat
Fromm	Performance	1. poultry by-products 2. poultry by-product meal 3. oatmeal 4. rice 5. corn
	Lite	1. poultry by-products 2. poultry by-product meal 3. oatmeal 4. rice 5. corn

Company	Food	Ingredients
Hill's Pet Nutrition	Science Diet Light	1. corn 2. soybean mill run 3. peanut hulls 4. poultry by-product meal 5. dried whey
Iams	Mini Chunks	1. chicken by-product meal 2. corn 3. rice 4. animal fat 5. beet pulp
Iams	Eukanuba Original	1. chicken by-product meal 2. corn 3. chicken 4. rice 5. chicken fat
	Lamb Meal & Rice for Puppies	1. lamb meal 2. rice flour 3. fish meal 4. corn 5. sorghum
Kal Kan Pedigree	Mealtime with Rice & Vegetables	1. corn 2. meat and bone meal 3. rice 4. wheat 5. wheat mill run
Kruse's Country Perfection	Adult	1. wheat 2. corn 3. beef and bone meal 4. soybean meal 5. chicken fat

FIGURE 14, CON'T.

Company	Food	Ingredients
	Puppy	1. wheat 2. corn 3. beef and bone meal 4. soybean meal 5. chicken meal
Natural Life	Puppy	1. brown rice 2. lamb meal 3. oatmeal 4. poultry fat 5. dried kelp
	Senior	1. corn 2. poultry meal 3. wheat 4. eggs 5. oatmeal
	Vegetarian	1. corn 2. rice 3. oatmeal 4. wheat 5. soybean meal
Nature's Recipe	Lamb Meal, Rice & Barley	1. lamb meal 2. brown rice 3. barley 4. lamb fat 5. lamb digest
	Senior/Pension Lamb Meal & Rice	1. brown rice 2. lamb meal 3. oats 4. wheat 5. soybean hulls
	Chicken Meal & Barley	1. chicken meal 2. brown rice

Company	Food	Ingredients
		3. barley 4. lamb fat 5. lamb digest
Nutro	Lamb & Rice Natural Choice	1. lamb 2. lamb broth 3. lamb liver 4. brewer's rice 5. egg
	Plus	1. chicken meal 2. rice 3. rice gluten 4. lamb meal 5. rice flour
Pet Products Plus	Mini Chunks Excell	1. chicken by-product meal 2. corn 3. brewer's rice 4. chicken fat 5. beet pulp
Purina	Dog Chow	1. corn 2. soybean meal 3. meat and bone meal 4. animal fat 5. corn gluten meal
	Hi Pro	1. corn 2. corn gluten meal 3. brewer's rice 4. meat and bone meal 5. soybean meal
Vet's Choice	Adult Lamb & Rice Select Balance	1. lamb meal 2. brewer's rice 3. wheat flour 4. poultry by-product meal 5. beet pulp

FIGURE 14, CON'T.

Company	Food	Ingredients
	Puppy Select Balance	1. corn 2. poultry by-product meal 3. animal fat 4. soybean meal 5. brewer's rice
Walthum	Adult Conditioning	1. rice 2. corn 3. chicken by-products 4. ground wheat 5. corn gluten
Wal-Mart	Ol' Roy	1. corn 2. soybean meal 3. meat and bone meal 4. wheat middlings 5. animal fat

FIGURE 15
FIRST FIVE INGREDIENTS
CANNED, SEMIMOIST AND FROZEN FOODS

Company	Food	Ingredients
Alpo	Prime Cuts in Gravy (canned)	1. water 2. beef 3. chicken 4. turkey 5. meat by-products
Friskies Pet Care Co.	Mighty Dog Senior Beef & Rice (canned)	1. water 2. meat by-products 3. beef 4. chicken 5. rice
Hill's Pet Products	Canine Senior Science Diet (canned)	1. water 2. chicken 3. meat by-products 4. rice 5. corn
Kal Kan Pedigree	Chopped Combo (canned)	1. water 2. meat by-products 3. poultry by-products 4. chicken 5. beef
Nutro	Lamb & Rice Natural Choice (canned)	1. lamb 2. lamb broth 3. lamb liver 4. brewer's rice 5. egg
Purina	Butcher's Burger Moist & Meaty (semimoist)	1. beef 2. soybean grits 3. corn syrup 4. corn flour 5. water

FIGURE 15, CON'T.

Company	Food	Ingredients
	Lean Moist & Meaty (semimoist)	1. soybean grits 2. corn syrup 3. corn flour 4. beef 5. water
Quaker Oats	Special Cuts Ken-L Ration (semimoist)	1. chicken 2. corn syrup 3. corn starch 4. soy flour 5. water
Ralph's Grocery Co.	Turkey & Bacon Aristocrat (canned)	1. turkey 2. water 3. bacon 4. salt 5. vegetable gums
	Gourmet Dinner Aristocrat (canned)	1. beef 2. water 3. deflourinated phosphate 4. salt 5. vegetable gums
Walter Kendall	Baked Loaf (frozen loaf)	1. beef by-products 2. wheat flour 3. meat and bone meal 4. wheat middlings 5. rice hulls
	Chicken Loaf (frozen loaf)	1. chicken 2. beef by-products 3. wheat flour 4. meat and bone meal 5. rice hulls

FIGURE 16
DRY FOOD PRESERVATIVES
AS LISTED ON THE LABEL

Company	Dog Food	Preservatives Used
Breeder's Choice	Maintenance	Mixed tocopherols/ ascorbic acid
Iams	Mini Chunks	BHA (butylated hydrox-yanisole)
Joy	Special Meal	BHA
Hill's Science Diet	Maintenance	BHA and citric acid
Kal Kan Pedigree	Mealtime	BHA
Kruse's Country Perfection	Adult	Ethoxyquin
Natural Life	Lamaderm	Vitamins E and C
Nature's Recipe	Chicken Meal	Vitamins E and C
Nutro Max	Puppy	Vitamins E and C
Super Pro	Adult	Mixed tocopherols
Vet's Choice	Select Lamb & Rice	Ethoxyquin
Walthum	Adult Conditioning	BHA

SIX

CHOOSING THE RIGHT FOOD FOR YOUR DOG

There are literally thousands of different dog foods available. There are canned foods, dry kibble, semimoist and frozen foods. Some foods are incredibly expensive and others are very cheap. There are very nutritious, complete dog foods made with ingredients approved for human use and other foods of dubious nutritional value with questionable ingredients. Some foods are nationally advertised while others are known in small geographic areas and promoted by word of mouth.

To make matters even more confusing, there are specialty foods: foods for dogs with specific needs. Almost all manufacturers have special foods for puppies, for adults and for older dogs. There are also diet foods for overweight dogs, special foods for pregnant or lactating bitches, high-calorie foods for working dogs and special foods for dogs with health problems.

How can you sift through this cornucopia of foods and narrow your selection down to one? Again, knowledge is key. Knowledge of the foods, what they are and what the terms mean.

Keep in mind, too, that many of the foods available are actually made for the dog's owner. David Mayberry of Iams Dog Foods said, "The varieties of flavors and imitation meats are aimed at the consumer and have no bearing on nutritional values." Dogs don't care whether or not their food is shaped like tiny dog bones, though many owners think they do.

CLASSIFICATIONS OF FOODS

There are three basic classifications of dog foods: economy, regular and premium. With today's sophisticated diets, these classifications have been further divided into economy, regular, premium, super-premium and performance.

Dog foods are thus classified because all are not created equal (although most manufacturers and their advertising firms would like to have you think so). The types of classification are not as important as why they exist and where the different foods fit into them. Let's look at each.

ECONOMY BRANDS

Dog foods that are listed in the economy classification are usually the generic-brand foods. You can buy them at grocery stores, feed stores or discount department stores. Economy foods are very inexpensive and are made of the cheapest ingredients available. As a result, they usually consist of poorer-grade ingredients. Their energy values are usually lower, as are their protein sources and digestibility. Even though the food may meet AAFCO's minimum nutritional requirements, that may not be enough for your dog.

The Veterinary Medical Teaching Hospital at the University of California, Davis, has identified what is being called "generic dog food–associated disease." This is, essentially, nutritional deficiencies that appear in dogs that have been fed economy-type dog foods. The disease or syndrome may show up as slow or retarded growth, skeletal abnormalities, poor hair coat, skin disorders—even behavior problems.

The Ralston Purina Company conducted studies in 1983 and 1984 and found that 83 percent of 73 different generic foods failed to meet the minimum established nutritional requirements for dogs. Not only that, but over half of those foods could not live up to the claims on their labels.

REGULAR BRANDS

Regular or mid-range dog foods are in the middle between economy and premium dog foods. These foods cost less than premium foods but more than economy. They have better-quality ingredients from better sources and are more digestible. These foods are often found at grocery stores, feed stores and some pet shops.

PREMIUM BRANDS

Premium foods, which include those foods also classified as super-premium and performance, use better-quality ingredients from sources with higher biological values. Consequently, their digestibility is higher. Whereas an economy or regular brand of dog food might use corn, wheat or soybeans as the primary ingredient, a premium quality food will be more likely to use a good-quality meat source as the main ingredient.

Because premium foods are made of better-quality ingredients and have better digestibility, dogs need to eat much less of them than they would of a lesser-quality food. Premium foods have another important advantage to many dog owners, and that is the fact that they produce less waste (less waste translates as less fecal matter to pick up in the yard).

FORMS OF FOODS, AND THEIR PROS AND CONS

Most dog foods come in one of four different forms:

1. dry
2. canned
3. semimoist
4. frozen

Dry food is the most popular form. Dry dog food usually has a moisture content of 10 percent or less and contains meats and meat products, grains, vegetables and other ingredients. Most dry foods are made using an extruder, a machine that can cook the food at a high temperature for a very short period of time. Dry dog foods are usually sold in bagged form, from four to 40 or 50 pounds per bag. The shelf life is normally three to six months, depending upon the method of preservation used.

Pros: Dry dog foods have a good shelf life, are easy to serve and store, and most are reasonable in price. There is no annoying odor, and the scraping action that takes place as the dog eats can assist in the dog's dental care.

Cons: The only drawback to dry food is that some dogs, especially those that have eaten canned or frozen foods, may resist eating it plain. For this reason, some owners add water or a spoonful or two of something else, like yogurt, to "spice up" the dry food.

Higher-quality **canned foods** are primarily meat products with a high moisture content, usually about 70 to 80 percent. Canned foods can and do contain other ingredients besides meat, some of which can be seen in the food (like peas and carrots), and others which are combined with other ingredients and are not as noticeable (like corn meal).

Pros: Canned foods are very palatable to the dog, especially the foods made primarily of meat. Canned foods also have a very long shelf life.

Cons: Canned foods do not help scrape tarter off your dog's teeth like dry foods can. Canned foods may also smell less than pleasant and, in the long run, can be more expensive than dry foods.

Semimoist foods are somewhere in between canned and dry foods in moisture content. Purina's Moist and Meaty Lean has a moisture content of 33 percent. Many of these foods list meat as one of the first five ingredients, but they also contain a variety of other ingredients, including sugar or sugar products. (Purina's Moist and Meaty Lean lists corn syrup as the second ingredient.)

Pros: These foods are usually packaged in individual servings, making them easy to store and easy to feed—they are very convenient.

Cons: As was previously mentioned, semimoist foods often contain great amounts of sugar, not a good source of nutrition for dogs. Semimoist foods are also more expensive than dry food, do not help with dental health and usually contain a number of artificial colors and preservatives.

Frozen foods (packaged in a loaf form) are very high in meat ingredients and in moisture content—about 60 to 70 percent. These can also contain other ingredients than meat, depending upon the food. The shelf life of these foods varies, depending upon the processing and the ingredients. The date is usually on the package. Cost also varies, depending upon the brand and the ingredients.

Pros: When thawed, frozen foods are very palatable and most dogs eagerly eat the food. Unused portions remain in the freezer, making them less likely to spoil.

Cons: Because the food is served thawed and soft, it does nothing to assist in your dog's dental care.

MIXING FOODS

Many dog owners mix dry and canned foods on a regular basis. Some owners feel that dry food is unappetizing or boring. Some dogs have convinced their owners that they will not eat plain dry food. Whatever the reason owners choose to mix dry and canned, some experts agree it's the better solution anyway.

Mike Guerber, a manager for Precise Pet Products, said, "Canned dog food is a very important part of canine nutrition." A study showed that the enzymes produced when dogs ate both dry and canned foods resulted in better digestion and utilization of both foods.

Guerber emphasized, though, that the foods should both be of high quality. "If you want to give your dog a premium dry food because of its superior nutrition, why would you want to dilute that with an inferior canned food?" A ratio of 75 to 80 percent dry food and 20 to 25 percent canned food seems to be an acceptable balance with most experts.

COST OF DOG FOODS

When comparing like forms of dog food—different brands of canned foods to each other, or dry foods to other dry foods—cost does often indicate quality. Because the ingredients needed for premium dog foods are of better quality, they cost more. The processing is usually of better quality, too. All of these costs are passed on to you, the consumer. Therefore, the premium dog foods do cost more.

In the long run, though, they are worth what you pay for them. Most dogs require less food when eating a premium brand because the food is more digestible. Nan Weitzman made a comparison in the article, "What's the Best Dog Food for Your Money?" (*Good Dog!* magazine, Jan./Feb. 1992). She stated that a 70-pound Irish Wolfhound would have to eat at least twelve cups of a dry economy brand dog food at 64 cents a day to compare with eating five cups of a premium brand food at 62 cents a day. Add that to the health benefits afforded by a better-quality food, plus fewer stools in the backyard, and a premium-quality food is obviously a better bargain.

FOODS FOR ALL AGES AND SIZES

PUPPY FORMULAS. Growth (puppy) foods are made by most of the larger dog food manufacturers. A puppy food should supply enough nutrition for growth, play and good health. Most of these foods are made with higher protein levels than adult formulas, generally from 24 to 28 percent. Fat levels are also higher, usually from 10 to 18 percent.

Most puppy foods also contain supplements of vitamins and minerals. However, keep in mind that more of these substances is not always better. As was mentioned in Chapter Four, oversupplementation of vitamins A, D, K and E can cause toxicity. An imbalance of calcium and phosphorus can have disastrous results. Therefore, read the label, look for a balance in the food, study the AAFCO chart for puppy food (see Figure 1 again) and don't hesitate to call the manufacturer if you have questions.

ADULT FORMULAS. Maintenance or adult foods should meet the needs of the majority of adult dogs. This food is for the so-called "average" dog, if there is really such a thing. An adult formula should supply enough calories for day-to-day living, exercise and good health.

The protein levels in most premium adult maintenance foods are usually between 18 and 24 percent, with fat levels between 8 and 12 percent. Again, vitamin and mineral supplementation is important, but if you have questions, call the manufacturer.

PERFORMANCE FORMULAS. Not all manufacturers offer a performance-type formula, but those that do have targeted their foods toward those dogs that are very active, under a lot of stress or working hard. Hunting dogs, police dogs, working livestock dogs and show dogs often need the higher protein and fat content of performance foods. Because these dogs are so active, they need more calories to supply their energy needs, to aid in good health and to combat stress.

Most performance foods offer protein and fat levels very much like puppy foods, from 24 to 28 percent (or even higher) for protein and from 10 to 18 percent for fat.

REDUCED CALORIE FORMULAS. Some experts have said that obesity is America's number-one health problem. Unfortunately, the same goes for America's dogs; more dogs are overweight today than ever before, and obesity can have some lasting effects on these dogs' health.

In response, a number of manufacturers are offering reduced calorie dog foods. Most of these foods offer reduced protein and fat levels and higher fiber. Protein averages 16 to 17 percent for most of the foods, with fat anywhere from 4 to 8 percent. The higher fiber levels (4 to 8 percent) serve a number of purposes, including keeping the bowels functioning well. The fiber also helps make the dog feel full, a benefit on any diet.

The challenge of any reduced calorie food is to provide adequate (or better!) nutrition while allowing the dog to feel full and cutting calories at the same time. A greatly reduced protein and fat percentage could hamper the dog's ability to thrive and remain active and healthy. Therefore, many veterinarians recommend feeding a premium food with at least 20 percent protein and 8 percent fat, then increasing the dog's daily exercise.

SENIOR/GERIATRIC FORMULAS. A debate is ongoing as to whether older dogs should eat less protein. One side of the argument states that senior dogs should have less protein as they age so that the kidneys and liver have to process less protein. The other camp argues that proteins are needed for energy, for tissue repair and for good health. Daniel Carey, DVM, Iams Dog Foods' director of technical communications, said, "A 1994 university study of protein and older dogs showed no adverse effects of protein on kidney function."

However, once a dog has kidney disease, most experts do agree that a lower-protein food is advisable. Also, as dogs age, their metabolism usually slows down and, as a result, many older dogs gain weight even when they are eating a food that has served them well all along. In these cases, reduced calories are a good idea.

If you're not sure whether your dog should eat a senior or geriatric food, call the manufacturers of the foods you are examining, tell them about your dog and ask them about their food. Also, talk to your veterinarian and get his or her input.

PRESCRIPTION DIETS. These diet formulas are called prescription or therapeutic diets because they are sold through veterinarians. They are formulated as nutritional aids for specific health problems, including heart disease, renal failure, pancreatitis, diabetes, gastrointestinal disorders, skin disease and more.

Several companies make prescription diets. Hill's Pet Nutrition, maker of Science Diet foods, makes a line called Prescription Diet. Pro Plan makes Clinical Nutrition Management and Vet's Choice makes Select Care nutritional aids.

The decision to put your dog on one of these diets should be made with your veterinarian. Not only is the food sold through your veterinarian, but some of these diets are quite different and your vet should monitor your dog as you change its food.

FIGURE 17
ECONOMY—PREMIUM FOOD COMPARISON

Economy Food	Premium Food
Lower purchase price	Higher purchase price
Primary Ingredients: corn, wheat, soybeans	Primary Ingredient: good-quality meat product
Low biological value	Higher biological value
Poor digestibility	Higher digestibility
Large feces	Smaller, firm stools
Low energy value	Higher energy value
Often makes claims: "For all life stages" "Meaty flavor" "Looks like . . ."	Claims are easily proven. Ingredients are set.
Ingredients can change depending upon market availability.	

FIGURE 18
ASSESSING YOUR DOG'S NUTRITIONAL NEEDS:
A WORKSHEET

The purpose of this worksheet is to help you decide upon the dog foods that meet or satisfy your needs as a responsible dog owner, as well as your dog's individual nutritional needs. By answering the questions as honestly as possible (no one will see it but you!), you can then analyze the foods available and choose the best food for you both.

YOUR NEEDS:

Do you have any particular concerns about the quality of dog food ingredients?_____

Are there any preservatives, chemicals or artificial colors you would rather your dog not eat?_____

Are there any food ingredients you would like to avoid?_____
_____

Are there any ingredients you would like your dog to eat?_____
_____

Is cost of the dog food a factor?_____

If price is important, what are you willing to spend?_____

Analysis: Make sure you understand how to read the labels on dog food packages so that you can choose a food of high quality with good ingredients so that you can include or exclude particular ingredients. Call the manufacturer if you have questions about particular ingredients, preservatives or additives. Keep in mind that it may not be possible to combine your philosophical beliefs with your dog's nutritional needs.

YOUR DOG'S HEALTH:

Is your dog of a breed that has known genetic disorders that affect or can be affected by food?_____

Is your dog a member of a breed with specific, known nutritional needs?_____

Has your dog been seen by its veterinarian within the last six months?_____

What is your dog's state of health today?_____

Does the dog have any ongoing health problems?_____

Could any of these be diet-related?_____

Could a special diet help ease any of these problems?_____

Does your dog have any confirmed or suspected food allergies?_____

    If yes, what are they?_____

Is your dog going to be bred?_____

Analysis: Make sure you have a good working relationship with your dog's veterinarian and talk to him or her about your dog's nutritional needs. As we have learned in previous chapters, diet can have significant effects on a dog's health.

We know, too, that specific breeds sometimes have different requirements. If your breeder and veterinarian cannot help you with information about your breed, you may wish to contact the national breed club, through the American Kennel Club. Or get a copy of William Cusick's book *Choosing the Best Food for Your Breed of Dog.* (See the Bibliography.) Also, a pregnant or lactating bitch needs specific nutrients from her food.

YOUR DOG'S AGE:

How old is your dog?_____

Could your dog benefit from an age-related specialty food, such as puppy food or senior food?_____

Analysis: There are many age-specific foods available and these formulations are certainly something to consider when choosing a food. However, age is not the only factor; instead, it is simply one piece of your dog's nutritional puzzle. Many, many puppies have grown up and thrived on adult dog foods and many older dogs have never eaten a bite of senior food.

YOUR DOG'S ACTIVITY LEVEL:

How much exercise does your dog get on a daily basis?_____

Does your dog participate in any working activities on a regular basis? (Herding, police work, guide dog, etc.) _____

Does your dog participate in dog shows? Herding trials? Flyball competitions? Other dog sports?_____

Does your dog have a lean body type combined with a constantly busy personality?_____

Analysis: Many dogs can maintain an active life while eating a premium brand, adult maintenance formula food. However, performance foods are available for dogs under stress, especially hard-working dogs. These higher-calorie, nutrient-dense foods might be appropriate for a very active or stressed dog.

YOUR DOG'S EMOTIONAL HEALTH:

Does your dog have any behavior problems?_____

Does your dog enjoy its training sessions?_____

How does your dog handle stress?_____
Is your dog often irritable? Depressed? Aggressive? Unpredictable?

_____

Is your dog mentally alert, bright-eyed and happy?_____

Analysis: Food allergies can cause a number of different problems, ranging from scratching and red skin to emotional and behavior problems and excessive mood swings. Ask your veterinarian for a referral to an allergist.

FIGURE 19
TOP-SELLING DOG FOODS AND TREATS

These were the top sellers of dog food according to an article in *Petfood Industry* magazine(July/August 1994).

Brand	Manufacturer	Dollars
Dry Foods:		
Dog Chow	Ralston Purina	$245 million
Puppy Chow	Ralston Purina	140 million
Mealtime	Kal Kan	100 million
Canned Foods:		
Pedigree	Kal Kan	$245 million
Alpo	Alpo	142 million
Mighty Dog	Friskies	91 million
Soft-dry/Semimoist:		
Kibbles N Bits	Quaker Oats	$133 million
Moist & Meaty	Purina	32 million
Tender Chops	Quaker Oats	24 million
Treats:		
Milk Bones	RJR-Nabisco	$138 million
Jerky Treats	Heinz	55 million
Cheweez	Friskies	53 million

FIGURE 20
TASTE TESTS

I conducted these tests with my dogs for my own information, wanting to check the appeal and palatability of some of the foods. These tests are unscientific, although it was fun to watch the dogs' reactions. To conduct each test, I put the dog in another room while I set out the foods or treats. I placed each food in a small pile in a semi-circle so that when I brought the dog to a specific spot, each food would be within reach and the same distance from the dog. I brought the dog in for the test, had it sit in the prearranged spot, then told the dog, "Okay! Get the treat!" and let the dog go to the food it wished. In most cases, the dog sniffed first, tasted one or two and then started to eat one food.

Assorted Dry Foods

Test Dog: Dax, a year-old Australian Shepherd who can be very picky with her food.

Foods offered:

> Select Balance Adult Lamb Meal & Rice
> Natural Life Vegetarian
> Nature's Recipe Chicken Meal, Rice & Barley
> Nutro Max Mini Size
> Pedigree Mealtime Rice & Vegetables
> Advanced Pet Diets Lamb Meal & Rice

Dax chose: Nutro Max Mini Size, with no hesitation, and proceeded to eat the entire sample.

Adult/Maintenance Dry Foods

Test Dog: Ursa, an eight-year-old Australian Shepherd, a proverbial "food hound."

Foods offered:

> Natural Life Lambaderm
> Excell Mini Chunks
> Dick Van Patten's Natural Balance
> Iams Mini Chunks
> Sensible Choice Lamb and Rice, Adult
> Sensible Choice Chicken and Rice, Adult

Ursa chose: Natural Life Lambaderm, and tried to swallow the entire sample when I went to pick it up.

Less Active/Reduced Calorie Dry Foods

Test Dog: Ursa, who with her love of food is often on a reduced calorie diet.

Foods Offered:

> Vet's Choice Select Balance Less Active
> Sensible Choice Lamb Meal & Rice, Reduced
> Eukanuba Light

>   Advanced Pet Diets Lite
>   Science Diet Light

Ursa chose: In a rare discriminating moment, Ursa sniffed but did not eat a couple of the foods. She finally chose Eukanuba Light.

Performance Dry Foods

Test Dog: Dax
  Foods Offered:
>   Natural Life Condition
>   Nutro Natural Choice Plus
>   Eukanuba Original
>   Proper Balance Super Premium
>   Purina Hi Pro

Dax chose: Natural Life Condition, but only after sniffing all the samples.

Puppy/Growth Formulas

Test Dog: Care Bear, my ten-year-old Australian Shepherd. He wouldn't ordinarily eat puppy food since he has been on a senior diet for a year or two. This was a treat.
  Foods Offered:
>   Eukanuba Puppy
>   Nutro Max Puppy
>   Advanced Pet Diets Growth
>   Natural Life Puppy
>   Excell Puppy
>   Country Perfection Puppy
>   Nutro Natural Choice Puppy
>   Sensible Choice Lamb & Rice Puppy
>   Select Balance Puppy

Bear chose: Eukanuba Puppy and Natural Life Puppy. He inhaled them both equally fast.

SEVEN

FEEDING YOUR DOG

This may seem like the simplest and most obvious part of providing for your dog's eating needs, but it, too, can be confusing. There are choices to be made about:

1. when to feed your dog
2. where to feed your dog
3. how much to feed your dog
4. how often to feed your dog
5. how to evaluate your dog's food
6. what to do about changing your dog's food.

All these things contribute to your dog's overall health.

Keep in mind that you should feed your dog yourself, fixing its food and putting the food down in front of it. If you have more than one dog, feed each dog its own food in its own bowl and don't let them switch. This way you know each dog got the right food. You also know which ate how much (or how little), how quickly (or slowly), which left food in its bowl and which didn't eat at all. After all, a change in appetite is one of the first signs of illness in many dogs.

WHEN TO FEED

This will depend on your dog's age and your lifestyle. If you have a puppy, you'll need to feed it three or four times a day until the puppy is about six months old. These meals should come about four to six hours apart and will be given in conjunction with the puppy's housetraining schedule. For example, if puppy gets up at 7 AM and is fed at 7:30, its next meal can be around noon, then again at 5:30 or 6 PM, depending on your schedule. Whatever times you choose, be consistent. Puppies thrive on a routine, and it makes housetraining much easier.

Adult dogs can be fed around their owners' schedules, usually once in the morning and once in the evening. Don't feed too close to bedtime, and don't feed immediately before or after vigorous exercise. Like puppies, adult dogs thrive on a routine, so stick to regular mealtimes! (See "How Often to Feed?" below)

If your family's and your dog's mealtimes are approximately the same, your family should eat first. In the wild, the leaders of the wolf pack have first shot at a meal, and though your dog is not a wolf, your family is still its "pack," and eating after you is one more way to establish pecking order. If your family eats late in the evening, however, don't make your dog wait. Discourage begging habits at all times by keeping your dog in a separate room while you eat, or asking it to sit or lie down away from the table.

WHERE TO FEED

Your puppy or dog should have a quiet place to eat. Food and water bowls should be put in the same place every day. Choose a corner of the kitchen or a pantry or hallway where your dog can fit comfortably and enjoy its meal relatively uninterrupted. An area where people are constantly coming and going is not a good spot; all the activity will distract the dog from the meal, and may cause it to gulp the food anxiously or ignore it. If you have more than one dog, feed them together, but give them enough room so they don't feel territorial about their bowls. Watch so that the dog that eats faster doesn't eat the slower dog's meal.

Though you want to feed your dog in a quiet place, you don't want to train it to be possessive about the food bowl. Any family member should be able to approach the dog while it's eating and even take the bowl away if necessary. Good manners need to be trained. Every so often, feed your dog its dinner from the bowl (if you mix in canned food, leave it out this time and replace it with something you don't mind touching, like small pieces of chicken or cheese). This is a good time to train your dog to take food gently, too.

HOW MUCH TO FEED

The label on the dog food, regardless of type, will list suggested feeding amounts. For example, the label on Iams Natural Lamb Meal and Rice Formula (dry food) says that a 10- to 20-pound dog should eat 1-1/4 to 2 cups per day. This is a premium brand, and as a general rule, the dog being fed this nutrient-dense food will need to eat significantly less of it than of economy brand food. Each brand's label will have feeding instructions, which is why they'll vary.

But for most dogs, the suggested feeding amounts are just the starting point in figuring out how much they should actually eat. In fact, a product's suggested amounts are sometimes way off what an individual dog really needs. So how will you know how much to feed your dog? Ask yourself these questions:

- How active is your dog? Activity level definitely affects how much food it needs. A very active dog will need more calories than a dog eating the same food but sleeping on the couch. Activities vary, too, from running around the yard chasing squirrels to jogging or biking with you to performing a specific task like sledding, herding or hunting.
- What kind of climate do you live in? Weather also affects how much food a dog will need. Dogs that spend any time outside in cold weather will need more calories to keep warm. Dogs in a warm climate may not have to worry about keeping warm, but may expend energy keeping cool or lose more calories while working.
- Does your dog get treats and scraps regularly? Be honest! The dog that is regularly fed treats, snacks or scraps between meals will need less food. You should think of treats as a portion of your dog's daily diet and factor them into the total amount you feed. Dogs like treats and owners like giving them, so you probably won't want to eliminate them altogether. However, feeding scraps can also destroy the nutritional balance of a good-quality commercial food and often leads to obesity. Be conscientious about what kind of treats and scraps you feed, as well as how much and how often you feed them.

You can weigh your dog to see if it's losing or gaining weight, or you can just tell by looking at or touching it. Adjust the feeding amounts accordingly.

HOW OFTEN TO FEED

Puppies should eat three times a day, with the largest meal in the morning. Small or toy breed puppies have a tendency toward hypoglycemia, and as a result, might even need to eat four times a day.

Even though it seems to be traditional to feed adult dogs once a day, most dogs do better on two meals, with the larger meal in the morning. Dogs fed once a day have a tendency to beg—because they are hungry—and often get irritable because of hunger or low blood sugar.

EVALUATING THE RESULTS

After your dog has been eating a food for four to six weeks, you can evaluate the results to see if they are what you want. Evaluate your dog by answering the following questions:

- Does your dog's coat look healthy? Are the hairs shiny and full? Brittle and dull?
- Is your dog's skin smooth and pliant? Dry and scaly? Blotchy or itchy?
- Are your dog's eyes bright and alert?
- Is your dog at a proper weight, neither too fat nor too thin? (For the average dog of proper weight, you should be able to feel ribs below skin without them showing too much through the skin.) Is your dog eating all its food?
- Is your dog's activity level normal or better than it used to be? Does your dog want to run and play?
- When you are practicing obedience training, is your dog mentally alert? Does it learn easily and retain what it has learned?
- Are your dog's stools firm, dark (but not black) and with relatively little odor?

If your dog's coat, skin and eyes appear clean, clear and blemish-free, and if it is eating well and has a good activity level, it should be getting the nutrition it needs from the food. If there is a problem with any of the answers, you may wish to look again at the food your dog is eating. If you have any doubts, talk to your veterinarian, as any difficulties may indicate an underlying health problem.

CHANGING YOUR DOG'S FOOD

If you decide to change the food you are feeding your dog, don't do so abruptly. Some dogs will refuse to eat when their food is changed and others will suffer severe gastrointestinal upset, complete with diarrhea and vomiting. Changes in a dog's diet must be made gradually.

Start making the change prior to running out of the dog's old food. When you have about three weeks of food left, buy some of the new food. For the first week of the change, feed three-quarters old food and one-quarter new food. For the second week of the change, feed half old food and half new food. And finally, during the third week, feed one-quarter old food and three-quarters new food. By the fourth week, you can feed the new food entirely.

EIGHT

SUPPLEMENTS FOR DOGS: SHOULD YOU OR SHOULDN'T YOU?

Most nutritionists and veterinarians consider a supplement to be anything that is added to the dog's diet on a regular basis. Therefore, if you add some yogurt to your dog's food each day, that is a supplement. If you add a multi-vitamin/mineral tablet, that too is a supplement. There are a number of other supplements that are commonly used by dog owners, some commercial preparations, others homemade.

Should you use supplements? As with so many aspects of canine nutrition, the experts' opinions vary. Some, especially those researchers working with dog food manufacturers, say that a good-quality food is all a dog needs. Dr. James Sokolowski and Dr. Anthony Fletcher, authors of *Basic Guide to Canine Nutrition* (Gaines Professional Services), state that when a dog is fed a dog food that is labeled "complete and balanced," supplements should only be given to correct a specific dietary need, such as the dog's inability to digest or metabolize certain nutrients.

However, many other experts say that even a "complete and balanced" dog food is not always enough, that it doesn't take into consideration each dog's individual needs and the actual quality and digestibility of the dog food.

Richard Pitcairn, DVM, states in his book, *Dr. Pitcairn's Complete Guide to Natural Health for Dogs and Cats* (Rodale Press, 1982), "I always recommend the inclusion of several nutrition-packed food supplements in the [dog's] diet." He continues by saying that those supplements are recommended because they fortify the diet with plenty of important vitamins and minerals. A dog's diet may be lacking in nutrition due to soil depletion as well as storage and cooking procedures.

Dr. Pitcairn also believes that the stress and pollution we take for granted as part of modern life can cause nutritional deficiencies.

Dr. Clarence Hardin, Director of the California Mobile Veterinary Service and a well-known preventative medicine vet, recommends a number of dietary supplements. He says, "Today's dogs face a number of critical health dangers, including air and water pollution and substandard, chemically laden dog foods. Often traditional nutrition and medicine are not enough."

Other experts recommend supplements for specific situations, such as for hard-working dogs, dogs under stress or those with health problems. Supplements of specific types are also often recommended for dogs with health disorders, especially diseases affecting nutrition or digestion.

DECIDING TO SUPPLEMENT

Deciding what supplements to add to the dog's diet is often difficult. Many dog owners give their dogs the same vitamin, mineral or herbal supplements they themselves use. Other dog owners hear or read about a supplement that is supposed to accomplish something specific, such as produce healthy skin, and they start adding that to their dogs' diets.

As long as the supplement itself is not harmful to the dog, and the amount given is appropriate to the dog's size, condition and general health, the only real danger with supplementing a diet is that the supplement may unbalance a previously balanced, complete food. However, most experts agree that if commercial supplements are given according to directions and homemade supplements do not total over 10 percent of the food eaten, they are probably safe.

When giving supplements, it is important that the dog's overall condition and health are watched closely. If there appears to be any kind of allergic reaction, stop the supplement and call your veterinarian. If there is any detrimental change in the dog's condition or health, again, stop the supplement and talk to your veterinarian.

Keep in mind, too, that if you are trying to accomplish something specific with the supplement, such as improve skin and coat condition, food supplements take time to work. It may take a few weeks before you see any change in your dog's skin, and even two to three months before you see any change in the dog's coat.

COMMERCIALLY AVAILABLE SUPPLEMENTS

ENZYME FORMULAS. Enzyme formulas are designed to enhance or replace naturally occurring enzymes. Pancreatic enzymes are often recommended as supplements for dogs that no longer produce enough enzymes on their own. Other enzyme supplements are derived from plant sources, such as papain or bromelain.

Enzyme supplements can be especially beneficial when a dog is on a high-fiber diet. Fiber is known to interfere with zinc absorption in the intestinal tract, and additional enzymes can free up those and other nutrients in the fiber, making them easier for the dog to metabolize.

One popular formula, Prozyme, is advertised as "Enhancing the bioavailability of all pet foods." It is supposed to work directly on the food by replacing the natural enzymes lost due to processing.

FATTY ACID FORMULAS. There are a number of fatty acid supplements available commercially and most are advertised as beneficial to the skin and coat. Most are formulated to be high in essential fatty acids, especially linoleic and arachidonic acids. These are usually recommended for dogs with skin allergies or other disorders, including dietary deficiencies, that are causing poor hair coat, dry skin or excessive shedding.

VITAMIN/MINERAL SUPPLEMENTS. There are probably as many vitamin/mineral supplements available for dogs as there are for people. Dog owners can purchase complete vitamin/mineral preparations or they can buy supplements containing one specific vitamin or mineral.

When supplementing a commercial food, it's important to know what vitamins and minerals the food contains and in what amounts, because with many vitamins and minerals, too much is just as dangerous as too little. If you are in doubt as to what your dog is getting from its food, call the dog food manufacturer and ask.

Sometimes individual vitamins or minerals are recommended for a specific purpose. Figures 10 and 12 in Chapter Four discuss vitamin and mineral deficiencies (as well as excesses) and can serve as a guideline as to what you may want to supplement.

Source Plus! Micronutrients is a commercially available product that is derived from dehydrated seaweeds and contains over 60 different vitamins, macrominerals and microminerals (trace minerals). The literature for Source Plus! states, "All 50 states in the United States have reported mineral deficiencies in farmland soils, deficiencies which work their way up the food chain into the diets of horses, dogs and humans."

Food Supplements. A few supplements are available that are made from foods rather than simpler food forms such as vitamins, minerals, fatty acids or enzymes. Most of these supplements are designed to provide more complete nutrition for dogs, aiding what might otherwise be a less than complete diet.

#1 All Systems, a company known for its grooming products, has produced a supplement called Vital Energy. Made from flax seed, molasses, yeast, rice bran, liver, alfalfa and a number of other quality ingredients, Vital Energy contains antioxidants, phytochemicals, enzymes, amino acids, trace minerals and vitamins. Vital Energy is itself a balanced food, eliminating the concern of oversupplementation.

HERBAL SUPPLEMENTS

Herbs have been used as nutritional supplements and as preventative and curative medicine for thousands of years. Thanks to antibiotics, aspirin and other "magic bullet" medicines, the use of herbs decreased over the last century. However, people have discovered that those magic bullets are not all-powerful, and the use of herbs has increased significantly over the last decade.

Again, as with many aspects of canine nutrition, the experts—nutritionists, veterinarians and researchers—disagree on the use of herbs as supplements. Some are outspoken in their beliefs that the powers of herbs are, literally, "old wives' tales." Others answer back that those old wives kept mankind and mankind's domestic animals alive for thousands of years prior to the dawn of modern medicine.

The herbs listed below are those whose use is more widely accepted. If you or your veterinarian has any questions as to dosage and side effects, or if you simply want more information, check with your local health food store or see the bibliography in the back of this book for further reading on the subject.

Alfalfa (which means "the father of all foods") is full of trace minerals and vitamins A, E, K, B and D. It has also been used to alleviate the pain and stiffness of arthritis and the discomfort of stomach ailments.

Red Clover is a stimulant for healing and is good for a recuperating or older dog.

Dandelions are known to help the body filter toxins from the system.

Echinacea is an herb known by experts to stimulate the immune system, so much so that physicians are even recommending it to patients during flu season.

Garlic has antibacterial, antifungal and antiviral properties. Whole books have been written about the wonders of garlic. Garlic boosts the immune system and stimulates the internal organs, especially the liver and colon, helping to rid the body of toxins.

Ginseng is often called a wonder drug. This root is known to strengthen the heart, builds general mental and physical vitality and stimulates the endocrine glands, which control the body's systems. Ginseng is a preventative, which means it is not given as medicine but rather as a daily supplement.

Rose Hips are really not herbs in the true definition but are instead the seed pods left after a rose blossom passes by. Rose hips are full of vitamins, including A, B, E, K and more vitamin C than any other food we know—even more than citrus fruits. However, rose hips should only be used when they are free of insecticides, fertilizers and fungicides.

ESPECIALLY GOOD FOODS

Many foods are known to have special nutritional significance; others are known to have medicinal properties. As with herbs, experts disagree as to exactly how important these foods are. Again, if you want more information, or have any doubts, ask questions at your local health food store, talk to your veterinarian or check the bibliography of this book for more information. Listed below are foods whose properties are more widely known and accepted.

Apples—We have all heard the saying "An apple a day keeps the doctor away." Does that apply to dogs as well? Some experts think so. Apples are packed with chemicals that have been shown to kill cancers in animals. Apples also inhibit infectious disease and stabilize blood sugar. A slice or two of fresh apple makes a great treat that many dogs will eagerly devour for the fruit's sweetness.

Barley is a grain and has recently been used more frequently in dog foods. Barley is known to improve bowel function and is thought to possibly inhibit cancer.

Broccoli is known to inhibit cancer and is also a great source of many vitamins, including vitamin A.

Carrots are a wonderful source of beta carotene, but they contain other vitamins and trace minerals as well.

Cranberry Juice is known to have beneficial effects on the urinary tract, preventing infections and cystitis. Cranberry juice is also recognized as having strong antiviral properties.

Fish, especially saltwater fish, have a number of nutritional benefits. Ingestion of as little as one ounce of saltwater fish daily is known to boost the immune system, inhibit cancer, combat kidney disease and increase mental alertness.

Kelp is a type of seaweed. It is usually sold dried and ground to a fine powder, often encased in gel capsules. Kelp is an excellent mineral supplement as it is high in iodine, calcium and potassium as well as other trace minerals. Kelp is also known to boost the immune system and kill bacteria.

Yeast is a well-known food supplement; in fact, many dog foods contain yeast as a primary ingredient. Yeast are fungi grown in a fermentation of carbohydrates and are high in vitamins and minerals, especially the B vitamins. Brewer's yeast is the most nutritious of the different kinds of yeast available.

Yogurt—Besides being a nourishing food on its own, yogurt contains beneficial bacteria that improve bowel function. These bacteria help prevent intestinal infections, prevent diarrhea and kill problem-causing bacteria. Yogurt is also known to boost the immune system and is thought to have anticancer properties.

IN CLOSING

Adding a supplement to your dog's food is a personal decision that should not be undertaken lightly. Too much supplementation can upset a previously balanced and complete diet. For example, raw eggs can hinder the absorption of biotin, a B-complex vitamin. Too much calcium and phosphorus can result in a myriad of health problems.

However, supplements added to the diet wisely can benefit your dog greatly; improving skin, coat, energy, stress resistance or overall health. The key to using supplements is to do so intelligently, researching the supplement and the food your dog eats. If you have any doubts, talk to the dog food manufacturer, and if the supplement you are adding is a commercially manufactured supplement, talk to that company's representative as well. If you see any detrimental changes in your dog's health, of course, stop the supplement immediately and call your veterinarian.

NINE

HOMEMADE DIETS

Dog owners who decide to cook for their dogs do so for a variety of reasons. Sometimes a dog will have specific needs—such as food allergies—that cannot be satisfied by commercial foods. Sometimes the dog owner wishes the dog to eat according to the owner's nutritional or philosophical beliefs. Or the owner might be concerned about the ingredients that commercial dog foods contain.

The decision to feed a homemade diet is not one to be taken lightly. Today's dog foods are the result of much research—sometimes years of laboratory analysis and feeding trials. Replacing that research with an indiscriminate homemade diet can result in nutritional disaster. Even some nutritionists are hesitant about formulating their own diets. However, if you feel strongly about feeding your dog a home-cooked diet, if care is taken and the dog's health is monitored closely, a homemade diet can work.

Change your dog over to a homemade diet slowly, over a period of three weeks. If you switch too quickly, your dog will suffer gastrointestinal upset, possibly including vomiting and diarrhea. The first week, feed three-quarters (75 percent) old food and one-quarter (25 percent) new food. The second week, feed fifty/fifty. The third week, feed one-quarter old food and three-quarters new food. By the fourth week, you should be able to feed the new diet entirely.

One pitfall of a homemade diet you should be aware of is that the diet is cooked and soft and therefore provides no chewing action, no gum stimulation and no dental benefits, except of course those benefits provided internally by good nutrition. You will have to provide something for your dog to chew (like chew toys or carrots) and you will have to pay attention to your dog's teeth, cleaning them on a regular basis.

MONITORING THE RESULTS

Just as with a commercial food, the test of the food is in the results it produces. If your dog has food allergies, you should start to see some change after about a week or two on the new diet. Your dog will not be "all better," but you should see some lessening of the symptoms. If the symptoms get worse or if new problems pop up, stop the new diet, go back to the old and call your veterinarian. You may need to adjust the contents; perhaps there is a food allergy you didn't know about.

Watch your dog's weight, too. Many dogs are so thrilled with the new diet they act absolutely famished and will overeat if given the chance. If your dog gains weight after starting the new diet, decrease the amount of food slightly.

Keep in mind that diet is important but it is not the only thing that affects your dog's health. Keep track of your dog's health and what happens in the dog's environment, and work with your veterinarian.

IN CLOSING

Figures 21 through 25 detail several different homemade diets. These were formulated by health-conscious dog owners or breeders who were concerned about the food their dogs were eating. These people were not, however, veterinarians or dieticians, although several did consult with experts while formulating their diets.

Other homemade diets are available from other sources, including *Pet Allergies: Remedies for an Epidemic*, by Dr. Alfred Plechner (Very Healthy Enterprises, 1986); *Dr. Pitcairn's Complete Guide to Natural Health for Dogs and Cats*, by Richard Pitcairn, DVM, Ph.D. and Susan Hubble Pitcairn (Rodale Press, 1982); and *The Holistic Guide for a Healthy Dog*, by Wendy Volhard and Kerry Brown, DVM (Howell Book House, 1995).

Please consult with your veterinarian before you start your dog on any homemade diet, watch your dog carefully as you feed this diet, and keep your vet posted about any changes you notice in your dog's skin, coat, energy level, teeth and overall health.

FIGURE 21
A BASIC HOMEMADE DIET

This is a basic diet for dogs with no known food allergies. Adjust the amounts depending upon your dog's appetite, activity level, energy needs and weight gain or loss.

Mix together in a big bowl:

1 pound ground meat (chicken, turkey, lamb) browned, drained of most of the fat

1 medium potato, cooked, mashed

2 cups cooked whole-grain brown rice

1/2 cup cooked oatmeal

1/2 cup cooked, mashed barley

1/2 cup grated carrots, raw

1/2 cup finely chopped raw green vegetables (broccoli, spinach, green beans)

2 tablespoons olive oil

2 tablespoons minced garlic

Store in the refrigerator in a covered bowl, or divide into daily servings and store in the freezer, thawing a day or two at a time.

Add one of the following when serving:

Yogurt (a teaspoon for a toy dog, a tablespoon for a medium dog)

A multi-vitamin/mineral supplement

Herbal supplements (depending upon your dog's needs)

FIGURE 22
HIGHER-CALORIE DIET

This higher calorie diet is good for hard-working dogs, pregnant or lactating bitches or dogs under stress.

Mix together in a large bowl:

1 pound ground meat, browned (do not drain off fat from chicken or turkey)

4 large eggs, hardboiled, shelled, crumbled

2 cups cooked whole-grain brown rice

1 cup cooked oatmeal

1 large potato, cooked, chopped

1/4 cup wheat germ

1/2 cup raw grated carrot

1/2 cup chopped raw green vegetables

3 tablespoons olive oil

2 tablespoons minced garlic

Refrigerate in covered bowl or divide into daily servings.

Add one of the following when serving:

Appropriate size spoonful of cottage cheese

Appropriate size spoonful of yogurt

Dash of dry powdered milk

Dash of yeast

A multi-vitamin/mineral tablet

Herbal supplements (depending upon your dog's needs)

FIGURE 23
A DIET FOR DOGS WITH FOOD ALLERGIES

Before starting this diet, you should have an idea of the foods to which your dog is allergic. You can have your veterinarian run allergy tests, or with your veterinarian's guidance, you can do some food elimination tests at home. Then, depending upon what your dog is allergic to, you can make this diet suit your dog's needs. Obviously, if your dog is allergic to chicken, feed ground lamb instead. If your dog is allergic to eggs, drop them from the recipe and use another protein source, such as a milk product.

This is a basic recipe; adjust the amounts of ingredients according to your dog's size, appetite and needs. Make substitutions depending upon your dog's allergies.

Mix together in a large bowl:

1 pound ground meat (chicken, turkey or lamb) browned, drain off all but a little of the fat

2 hardboiled eggs, crumbled

3 cups cooked whole-grain brown rice

1 cup cooked oatmeal

1/2 cup grated carrot, raw

1/2 cup chopped green vegetables, raw (broccoli, spinach, green beans)

2 tablespoons olive oil

1 tablespoon minced garlic

Store in refrigerator, or store the food in the freezer divided into daily portions and stored in plastic bags.

Add one of the following when serving:

Yogurt (a teaspoon for toy dogs, a tablespoon for medium dogs)

A multi-vitamin/mineral tablet

Herbal supplements (based upon your dog's needs)

FIGURE 24
ALTERNATIVE HYPOALLERGENIC DIET

This recipe is for dogs allergic to meats and grains or grain products.

Mix together in a large bowl:

5 large potatoes, chopped into small pieces and cooked

3 eggs, hardboiled, shelled, crumbled

1 cup grated green vegetables, raw

1 cup cooked beans, finely chopped (kidney, black, lima)

1/2 cup grated carrot, raw

2 tablespoons olive oil

1 tablespoon minced garlic

Store in covered bowl or divide into daily servings and store in the freezer.

Add one of the following when serving:

Yogurt (a teaspoon for a small dog, a tablespoon for a medium dog)

A multi-vitamin/mineral tablet

Herbal supplements (depending upon your dog's needs)

FIGURE 25
VEGETARIAN DIET

Some vegetarian dog owners would like their dogs to eat a similar diet. Other dogs are allergic to meats. No matter why you feed your dog a vegetarian diet, keep in mind that dogs are carnivores, meat eaters. A vegetarian diet is not natural to a dog, and nutritional deficiencies are common on vegetarian diets. This diet does not contain meat, but is not a true vegetarian diet because it does include eggs and milk products; however, these are important nutritional sources. It is important to discuss this diet with your veterinarian before feeding it, and supervise it closely while feeding.

Mix together in a large bowl:

3 cups cooked whole-grain brown rice

2 cups cooked oatmeal

1 cup cooked mashed barley

2 hardboiled eggs, crumbled

1/2 cup grated carrot, raw

1/2 cup grated green vegetables, raw

2 tablespoons olive oil

1 tablespoon minced garlic

Store in refrigerator in covered bowl or divide into daily servings and store in freezer.

At mealtime, add a portion of each of these:

Yogurt (a teaspoon for a small dog, a tablespoon for a medium dog)

Tofu (a tablespoon for a small dog, 2 tablespoons for a medium dog)

A dash of whole dried milk (as if you were adding salt and pepper)

A multi-vitamin/mineral supplement

Herbal supplements (depending upon your philosophies and your dog's needs)

TEN

COMMERCIAL TREATS

In 1993, over $964 million was spent on dog treats in the United States. Some treats are pure junk food, full of corn syrup, meat scraps and cereal fillers. Other treats are actually good nutrition. But all of these biscuits, cookies, training treats and chews—anything your dog eats—must be taken into account when considering the dog's overall nutrition.

CHEW TREATS. Hard chew treats improve the dog's dental health by giving the dog a chance to exercise the gums and scrape the teeth. Chew treats also satisfy the dog's need to chew, especially that of teething puppies.

A number of different types of treats are available. Rawhide-type chew treats are very common and can be found in supermarkets or pet stores. Made from cowhide, these chew treats can be plain or flavored with beef, chicken, cheese or hickory. They are shaped into bone, doughnut or bagel shapes or straight sticks, or can be chopped up and molded into different shapes.

Depending upon what it is cured with, rawhide is generally considered to be a safe chew treat if you supervise the dog as it is chewing. Supervision is necessary because many dogs will chew off large pieces and then try to swallow them, choking on the softened hide. Owner intervention is occasionally needed to remove the offending piece before this happens.

There are lots of other hard bone-shaped goodies available, some of which are made out of animal products, others from vegetable sources. The Booda company has produced a "dog bone" made entirely from corn products that absolutely will not interfere with the dog's diet or nutritional balance. The pieces of the chew bone simply pass through the dog's digestive tract unchanged and are eliminated in the feces.

SEMIMOIST TREATS. These treats are very palatable; dogs love them. However, semimoist treats, like semimoist dog foods, have a higher sugar content than other treats. They are usually higher in additives, too, especially artificial colors and flavors. If you are concerned with your dog's diet, make sure to read the labels on these treats.

BISCUIT-TYPE TREATS. Hard, biscuit-type dog treats are very popular, with both dogs and their owners. These treats come in every size, shape, color and flavor imaginable. Some treats are round; others are square. There are big treats, little treats, beef flavored, liver flavored; the list is unending.

Many of these treats are actually good nutrition, not as a complete food, but as a supplement to your dog's diet. For example, Hill's Science Diet Adult Maintenance Treats are made from corn, brewer's rice, poultry by-product meal and animal fat. Their guaranteed analysis is 20 percent protein, 10 percent fat, 7 percent fiber and 10 percent moisture.

SPECIAL TREATS. Because treats are such big business and because dog owners want to give their dogs something special, many companies have responded with special treats. One such product is called Frosty Paws. The box says, "It's not ice cream but your dog will think it is!" This frozen treat is made from dried whey, soy flour, animal and vegetable fat and gelatinized corn flour. It is served in a little plastic cup with a paper lid, just like single-serving ice cream. It may not be ice cream but dogs really do love it!

WHAT NOT TO FEED YOUR DOG

Most nutritionists agree that you should avoid or severely limit your dog's sugar intake. Sugar is empty calories to your dog, just as it is for people, and treats loaded with sugar are very poor nutrition.

Avoid chocolate, too. Chocolate contains caffeine and theobromine, which people can digest but dogs cannot. Different kinds of chocolate have different chemical contents. Five ounces of dark, bitter baker's chocolate could poison a 50-pound dog. Sweet milk chocolate, the kind in most candy bars, is not quite as lethal but it's still dangerous. For example, the lethal dose for a toy breed dog, say a seven-pound Papillon, might be a single 10-ounce candy bar.

Most veterinarians also recommend that dog owners do not give their dogs bones. Although it seems that chewing on bones should be natural for dogs, many veterinarians have performed innumerable surgeries to repair the intestinal tracts of dogs that have ingested sharp bone pieces. Safer alternatives, like rawhides, are preferred.

FIGURE 26
COMMERCIAL DOG FOOD TREATS
NUTRITIONAL COMPARISONS

Company	Name	First Five Ingredients
American Nutrition Protein 20% Fat 5% Fiber 4.5% Moisture 10%	VitaBone	1. wheat flour 2. poultry meal 3. wheat 4. meat & bone meal 5. corn
Hill's Science Diet Protein 20.5% Fat 10.5% Fiber 7% Moisture 10%	Adult Treats	1 corn 2. brewer's rice 3. poultry by-product meal 4. animal fat 5. cellulose
Iams Protein 27% Fat 14% Fiber 3% Moisture 11%	Biscuits for Puppies	1. wheat flour 2. chicken by-products 3. beet pulp 4. poultry digest 5. brewer's yeast
Kal Kan Pedigree Protein 8% Fat 5% Fiber 4% Moisture 12%	Biscrok	1. wheat flour 2. poultry by-product digest 3. sugar 4. calcium carbonate 5. ground wheat
Nabisco Protein 18% Fat 6% Fiber 4% Moisture 10%	Milk Bones	1. wheat flour 2. skim milk 3. meat & bone meal 4. poultry by-product meal 5. animal fat
Nutritreat Protein 22% Fat 3%	Max's Chicken Snacks	1. wheat flour 2. meat & bone meal 3. corn

Company	Name	First Five Ingredients
Fiber 5%		4. poultry by-product meal
Moisture 11%		5. carrots
Purina	Bonz	1. corn
Protein 11%		2. wheat flour
Fat 5%		3. beef & bone meal
Fiber 4%		4. soybean meal
Moisture 12%		5. glycerin

FIGURE 27
COMMERCIAL DOG FOOD TREATS: TASTE TESTS

I conducted these tests with my dogs for my own information to check the appeal and palatability of these treats. Consequently, the tests are unscientific, but it was interesting to watch what the dogs chose. You can conduct similar "tests" with your dog or dogs. They won't argue!

Test dog: Care Bear, a ten-year-old Australian Shepherd, a proverbial "food hound".

Treats offered:

> Authority Premium dog snacks
> Sojournier Farms Natural Sojos dog treats
> Mother Hubbard's P-Nutter Gourmet Cookies
> Mother Hubbard's Charcoal dog treats
> Nature's Animals Natural Lamb & Rice Biscuits

Treat chosen: Authority Premium dog snacks

Test Dog: Dax, a year-old Australian Shepherd and a somewhat more selective eater.

Treats offered:

> American Health Kennels Bark Bars
> Jan's Wow-Bow Health Biscuits
> Eukanuba Vet Diets Restricted Calorie Treats
> Iams Puppy Formula Biscuits

Treat chosen: Iams Puppy Formula Biscuits

BIBLIOGRAPHY

Ackerman, Lowell. "Dietary Supplements: Therapy for the Skin." *Dog World* (September 1994): 18–20.

American Association of Feed Control Officials. Georgia Department of Agriculture, Atlanta. 404-656-3637.

Anderson, Moira. "Food for Thought." *Dog Fancy* 18, no. 5 (April 1987): 50–55.

Arden, Darlene. "David Horowitz on Dog Food." *Dog World* 72, no. 10 (October 1987): 12, 77–80.

Becker, Ross. "What's Really in Dog Food?" *The Dog Food Book*, 2nd edition. Austin, TX: *Good Dog!* Magazine, 1995.

Braley, James. *Dr. Braley's Food Allergy and Nutrition Revolution*. New Canaan, CT: Keats Publishing, Inc., 1992.

Cargill, John. "Feed That Dog!" *Dog World* 78, nos. 7–10 (July, August and September 1993): 24–29, 10–16, 14–22.

Carper, Jean. *The Food Pharmacy*. New York: Bantam Books, 1988.

Cusick, William D. *Choosing the Best Food for Your Breed of Dog*. Aloha, Oregon: Adele Publications, Inc., 1990.

Dick Van Patten's Natural Balance Pet Foods, PO Box 7956-425, Canoga Park, CA 91309.

Donoghue, Susan. "Nutrition: Cancer Prevention and Treatment." *AKC Gazette* 111, no. 4 (April 1994): 20–21.

———. "Nutrition: Feeding Different Breeds." *AKC Gazette* 110, no. 6 (June 1993): 20–21.

———. "Nutrition: Gastrointestinal Disorders." *AKC Gazette* 110, no. 11 (November 1993): 18–19.

————. "Nutrition: Stressed Out Dogs." *AKC Gazette* 109, no. 8 (August 1992): 22–23.

————. "Nutrition: Vitamin and Mineral Supplements." *AKC Gazette* 110, no. 10 (October 1993): 22–23.

Ducommun, Debbie. "Dog Food Debate." *Dog Fancy* 25, no. 11 (November 1994): 41–45.

Dunn, T. J. Jr. "Food for Thought." *Dog World* 80, no. 4 (April 1995): 50–52.

Dunne, Lavon J. *Nutrition Almanac,* 3rd edition. New York: McGraw-Hill Publishing Co., 1990.

Gearhart, Martha. "Veterinary Viewpoint: Deciphering Pet Food Labels." *The Pet Dealer* 42, no. 7 (July 1993): 20–24, 84.

Geslewitz, Gina. "RX for Mealtime." *Pet Dealer* 42, no. 12 (December 1993): 54–60.

Ginsberg, Susan. "Pets Battle the Bulge." *Animals* (November/December 1991): 5–8.

Glinsky, Martin. "Pet Food Fallacies." *The Dog Food Book*, 2nd edition. Austin, TX: *Good Dog!* Magazine, 1995.

Guidry, Virginia Parker. "Looking at Labels." *Dog Fancy* 26, no. 5 (May 1995): 46–53.

Haas, Elson M. *Staying Healthy with Nutrition.* Berkeley, CA: Celestial Arts Publishing Co., 1992.

Hill's Pet Products, PO Box 148, Topeka, KS 66601. 913-354-8523.

The Iams Company, 7250 Poe Avenue, Dayton, OH. 1-800-525-4267.

Jacobsen, Roy M. *Aqua Vitae.* Fargo, ND: Christopher Lawrence Communications, 1987.

Kallfelz, Francis A. "Supplements: When Are They Necessary for Your Dog's Health?" *Dog Fancy* 21, no. 3 (March 1990): 52.

Kritsick, Steve. "Nutrition and Health: You Get What You Pay For." *AKC Gazette* 102, no. 11 (November 1985): 22–23.

Lang, Laura. "Evaluating Dog Foods." *AKC Gazette* 105, no. 10 (October 1988): 48–52.

Lanting, Fred L. *Canine Hip Dysplasia and Other Orthopedic Problems.* Loveland, CO: Alpine Publishing, 1980.

Lewis, Lon D. "Feeding: Methods, Types and Problems." *Bloodlines* (March/April 1993).

Long, Patricia. "The Vitamin Wars." *Health* (May/June 1993): 45–54.

Ludeman, Kate, and Louise Henderson. *Do-It-Yourself Allergy Analysis Handbook.* New Canaan, CT: Keats Publishing, Inc., 1979.

Nutro Products, Inc., 445 Wilson Way, City of Industry, CA 91744. 818-968-0532.

"Pet Food Industry 1993 Maxwell Report." *Pet Food Industry Magazine,* 36, no. 4 (July/August 1994).

Pet Food Institute and Nutrition Assurance Program, 1200 19th Street NW, Suite 300, Washington, DC 20036. 800-851-0769.

Phelps, Karen. "Canine Nutrition: Fads, Facts and Fallacies." *Dog World* 70, no. 1 (January 1985): 11, 87–93.

Pitcairn, Richard H., and Susan Hubble Pitcairn. *Dr. Pitcairn's Complete Guide to Natural Health for Dogs and Cats.* Emmaus, PA: Rodale Press, 1982.

Plechner, Alfred J., and Martin Zucker. *Pet Allergies: Remedies for an Epidemic.* Inglewood, CA: Very Healthy Enterprises, 1986.

Ralston Purina Company. "Studies Focus on Bloat Risk Factors." St. Louis, MO (March 1995).

Reynolds, Arleigh. "Water: A Dog's #1 Nutrient." *Mushing,* no. 33 (July/August 1993): 26–28.

———. "What's in the Bag?" *Mushing,* no. 34 (September/October 1993): 30–33.

Ryan, Thomas. "Zinc: A Precious Mineral." *Dog Fancy* 16, no. 8 (August 1985): 46–47.

Shaffer, Martin. *Life After Stress.* Chicago: Contemporary Books, Inc., 1983.

Shojai, Amy. "Beating Cancer." *Dog World* 80, no. 1 (January 1995): 24–26.

———. "From Concept to Can." *AKC Gazette* 111, no. 10 (October 1994): 48–52.

———. "Reading the Dog Food Label." *Dog World* 77, no. 9 (September 1992): 14–18.

Smith, Carin. "RX Therapeutic Diet." *AKC Gazette* 108, no. 10 (October 1991): 78–82.

Sokolowski, James H., and Anthony M. Fletcher. *Basic Guide to Canine Nutrition*, 5th edition. Chicago: Gaines Professional Services, 1987.

Source Micronutrients, Source, Inc., 101 Fowler Road, N. Branford, CT 06471. 203-488-6400.

Thurston, Mary. "Dog Food Around the World." *Good Dog!* 6, no. 1 (January/February 1993).

———. "Feeding Fido in the Good Old Days." *Dog World* 77, no. 6 (June 1992): 14–20.

Vital Energy #1 All Systems, PO Box 1330, Ojai, CA 93023. 805-525-7998.

Volhard, Wendy, and Kerry Brown, DVM. *The Holistic Guide for a Healthy Dog*. New York: Howell Book House, 1995.

Warzecha, Mary. "Canine Cuisine." *Dog Fancy* 22, no. 7 (July 1991): 67–70.

———. "The $100 Dinner." *Dog Fancy* 19, no. 4 (April 1988): 17–20.

Weitzman, Nan. "How to Buy Dog Food." *The Dog Food Book*, 2nd edition. Austin, TX: *Good Dog!* Magazine, 1995.

———. "What's the Best Dog Food for Your Money?" *Good Dog!*, January/February 1992.

Wilford, Christine. "Allergies." *Dog Fancy* 25, no. 5 (May 1994): 47–51.

Willard, Thomas. "What Are We Really Feeding Our Dogs?" *AKC Gazette* 109, no. 7 (July 1992): 46–49.

INDEX